THE EDUCATOR AND THE OLIGARCH
A TEACHER CHALLENGES
THE GATES FOUNDATION

Praise for
The Educator and the Oligarch

"A powerful and important book by one of the most courageous advocates for sanity and simple justice in our public schools."

- **Jonathan Kozol**

"This book is a record of Anthony Cody's valiant struggle to force the nation's most powerful foundation and richest person to listen to the voice of an experienced teacher."

- **Diane Ravitch**

"A stick of chalk, the attendance list, and *The Educator and the Oligarch*. Anthony Cody's new book is a requirement for teachers in an era defined by the Gates Foundation's attempt to turn classrooms into a test prep centers. Anthony Cody, drawing on eighteen years as a classroom teacher, looks Bill Gates in the eye and announces that even he cannot buy our schools."

- **Jesse Hagopian, teacher, *Garfield High School, Seattle***

"Anthony Cody's book is a timely and concise reminder of just how much of a spoiled man's playground American public education has become to Gates and his profound net worth. Wealth should not be able to purchase a fundamental democratic institution. It is time for America to become much better educated about Bill Gates."

- **Mercedes Schneider, author, *Chronicle of Echoes***

"Anthony Cody's new book *The Educator and the Oligarch* is a brilliant, point by point challenge to Bill Gates role in undermining public education in the United States. What gives the book resonance and authority is Cody's own experience in grappling with every single issue that Gates raises from the standpoint of an innovative and caring science teacher in an Oakland middle school. But make no mistake about it- this book is also a call to arms against one of the greatest threats to Democracy I have seen in my lifetime. Bill Gates War on Public Education should alarm not only every American who cares about teaching and learning, but everyone who fears that the concentration of wealth at the top is eroding our best traditions. Anthony Cody gives us all the evidence we need to fight back, not only to save our schools, but to save our country."

- **Mark Naison, co-founder, *Badass Teachers Association***

"Anthony Cody has thought about education reform and those proponents whose wealth and power have been at the forefront of pushing the narrative that innovation comes from without and that teachers, students and parents just need to be compliant. His particular beef is with Bill Gates who has admitted that he and his foundation don't know whether "this will work". But in his attempt to use the very people who do the work with students to push his Master of the Universe agenda, Bill Gates runs smack dab into the heart of the issue. Anthony says "The trust teachers are given is a precious thing, and it obligates us to exercise our consciences and independent judgment." We must continue to fight for and be deserving of that trust."

- **Karen Jennings Lewis, President, *Chicago Teachers Union***

The Educator
And The Oligarch

A Teacher Challenges
The Gates Foundation

Anthony Cody

GARN
PRESS

New York, NY

GARN PRESS

NEW YORK, NY

Published by Garn Press, LLC
New York, NY
www.garnpress.com

Portions of this book were originally published by *Education Week Teacher (www. edweek.org/tm)* a publication of Editorial Projects in Education, and are reprinted by agreement. Views expressed do not reflect the opinions or endorsement of Editorial Projects in Education or any of its publications.

Book and cover design by Ben James Taylor/Garn Press

Library of Congress Control Number: 2014949049

Publisher's Cataloging-in-Publication Data
Cody, Anthony.
The educator and the oligarch : a teacher challenges the Gates Foundation / Anthony Cody.
     pages cm
     Includes bibliographical references.
     ISBN: 978-1-942146-00-1 (pbk.)
     ISBN: 978-1-942146-01-8 (e-book)
1. Privatization in education—United States. 2. Education and state. 3. Oligarchy. 4. Bill & Melinda Gates Foundation. 5. Business and education—United States.   I. Title.
     LB2806.36 .C63 2014
     379`.73—dc23
                                 2014949049

For my colleagues and students at Bret Harte Middle School in Oakland. We learned so much together.

Acknowledgements

This book was made possible by many people in my life. My wife, Randi, and my sons Alexander and Rowan, who bring me joy. My parents, Pat and Fred Cody, who modeled compassion and involvement every day. My editor at *Education Week's Teacher* magazine, Anthony Rebora. My many colleagues in Oakland, who made my career there so memorable. Eileen Engel, who helped me and many others in Oakland. Linda Darling-Hammond, who gave me some great opportunities and guided me to the National Board process. Misty Sato and Mike Atkin, who helped me improve as a teacher and thinker. Mary Porter, for her sharp insights, Denny Taylor for bringing this book to print. Diane Ravitch who has been an inspiration for us all. And all of those who are with me as we push for educational opportunities for all children.

Table of Contents

Preface

Anthony Cody is a teacher. For Cody, teaching is not just a job. It is his profession. It is his way of life. It is the place where his brain, his life experience, and his heart are joined. Having spent eighteen years as a middle-school science teacher in Oakland, California, having achieved National Board Certification while teaching in one of the nation's toughest urban districts, Cody embraces teaching as his mission in life. He now coaches teachers, mentors teachers, and tries to instill in them the love and spirit that animated his own teaching.

When Cody began blogging on a regular basis in *Education Week*, he called his blog "Living in Dialogue," which was an acknowledgement that truth is elusive and that there are usually at least two sides to every argument. Each column ends with pointed questions, inviting readers to agree or disagree with him, not to accept whatever he wrote as authoritative. He writes in the spirit of the science that he taught, with an informed mind, but with a skeptical bent, encouraging readers to question him and to question their own beliefs.

As a regular blogger, one with a particular interest in the teaching profession, it was only a matter of time until he began taking on the myriad of interest groups that are now seeking to undermine and destroy his beloved profession. He developed a large following, as he sharpened his ideas and his aims. In time, he recognized that the most powerful force in opposition to his own ideas about teaching was the Gates Foundation.

With his blog as his platform, he trained his sights on the Gates Foundation. While others feared to criticize the richest foundation in the United States, Cody regularly devoted blogs to questioning its ideas and programs. He questioned its focus on standardized testing. He questioned its belief that teachers should be judged by the test scores of their students.

He questioned its support for organizations that are anti-union and anti-teacher. He questioned its decision to create new organizations of young teachers to act as a fifth column within teachers' unions, ready to testify in legislative hearings against the interests of teachers and unions.

Perhaps because of his persistence, perhaps because of his earnest tone, perhaps because of his experience, Anthony Cody managed to get the attention of the Gates Foundation. The Foundation agreed to engage in a written debate with Cody. At the time, some of his admirers wondered whether the Gates Foundation would find a way to buy off or mollify or silence one of its most outspoken critics. But they underestimated Cody.

He exchanged several blogs with high-level members of the Gates Foundation, and his blogs were incisive, carefully documented, and fearless. The main point that he made—drawing on his own experience in Oakland as a classroom teacher but also on external and unimpeachable data—is that poverty is the greatest handicap to the academic performance of students today, not "bad teachers." He knew that the Gates Foundation had helped to fund the anti-teacher propaganda film "Waiting for 'Superman,'" and he saw the hand of the Foundation in almost every effort to reduce the status of the teaching profession and to replace it with scripts, standardized testing, and technology.

This book is a record of Anthony Cody's valiant struggle to force the nation's most powerful foundation and richest person to listen to the voice of an experienced teacher. Did Cody succeed? It is hard to know. Even as Cody was debating the Gates Foundation, it was spending billions of dollars to develop and implement the Common Core standards, which was yet another attempt to "teacher-proof" America's classrooms. Cody knows that past efforts at "teacher-proofing" the schools were never successful. He knows that good schools depend on teachers who are well prepared, devoted to improving their craft, and devoted to their students.

There is no replacement for well-prepared teachers or for a school where collaboration—not competition—is the norm. Cody also understands that teachers alone—no matter how good or great they are—and schools alone—no matter how good or great they are—cannot overcome the handicaps imposed on children, families and communities by inequality, poverty, and segregation. This is his message to the oligarch who runs the Gates Foundation: Will he listen?

Diane Ravitch

June, 2014

Introduction

I did not enter the arena to pursue Bill Gates. He and the other giants of corporate style reform came to me, in the school where I worked for 18 years.

When I was 29 years of age, I began working at Bret Harte Junior High in Oakland, and for the next 18 years I taught science, math and technology to a wonderfully diverse population of students. The year was 1987, and though *No Child Left Behind* was nowhere in sight, we knew we had a lot of work to do with our students.

My first few years I was involved in a project that prepared teachers in a variety of disciplines to engage our students in writing. Instead of old-fashioned research papers, I asked my students to be creative, and write science fiction stories in order to learn about the planets. After I took a workshop at the Exploratorium, I decided that doing hands-on experiments from carefully prepared teacher or textbook instructions was not very deep inquiry. I wanted my students to begin to see themselves as scientists – to feel agency -- not just follow a recipe handed to them. So I embarked in a year-long experiment with my own practice. I created dozens of different science investigation kits containing materials students could use to design their own experiments. I wanted them to work with the materials, then come up with their own questions and design experiments to answer them. This sort of inquiry is central to the scientific process.

I was disappointed when this open-ended approach did not work. The students were happy to mess around with the materials in their kits, but few experiments were done. So I went back to the drawing board, and came up with a more guided structure that met the students where they were. We all worked together with dry ice, and then they worked together to generate questions we could answer with experiments. The students then were able to design experiments and conduct them, and own the entire process.

My work with my colleagues was an experiment on a bigger scale. In the late 1990s, my principal approached me and suggested I apply for a grant to strengthen the science department. After consulting with my colleagues, we decided that our greatest concern was the high level of turnover in our department. Out of a department of ten, we were losing three or four teachers a year. With the funding, we paired the newer teachers with more experienced mentors, and held regular sessions. Members of the Math department were envious, so we expanded to include them in our second year. We were able to retain every single teacher in the department for several years. Our work deepened and moved beyond the basics into richer collaboration focused on shared assessments and Lesson Study.

This became the model for a district-wide mentoring program I created several years later, called *TeamScience*.[1] We organized veteran teachers to support their less experienced colleagues, and built a culture of sharing across the district.

But this work was an uphill battle, because the majority of science teachers Oakland was hiring were coming by way of Teach For America, or similar alternative credential programs. Many of the teachers entering on this pathway were not choosing teaching as a career. More than 75% were gone after three years.

My school struggled with the endless pressure to raise test scores, the constant threat that the students would not improve enough, and then the school would be closed, as were many Oakland schools.

And so it was that corporate reform came to my school and my district. The reformers came into professional organizations, and even the union to which I belonged. And they brought over and over again the message that my students, colleagues and the schools in which we worked, were failures, and needed to be replaced. My years there taught me well. I know they are wrong, and I am prepared to show why.

In the fall of 2010, an assault was unleashed on the teaching profession and the institution of public education in America. The assault was led by one of the wealthiest people on the planet, who was prepared to devote billions of dollars for a sustained campaign. This was the raw power of wealth at work.

The most visible vehicle was a highly charged documentary film, entitled *Waiting for Superman*. Bill Gates appeared in the film and issued a warning:

> We cannot sustain an economy based on innovation unless we have citizens well educated in math, science and engineering. If we fail at this, we won't be able to compete in the global economy. How strong the country is twenty years from now, and how equitable the country is twenty years from now, will be largely driven by this issue.[2]

The film also lionized Michelle Rhee, then chancellor of the Washington, DC, public schools, and Geoffrey Canada, founder of charter schools in Harlem. It identified teacher unions and due process as the source of problems for public schools, suggesting that "tenure" meant teachers had jobs for life and could not be fired. The overall message of the film was that if we overcome the resistance of teacher unions, fire the bad teachers, and open more charter schools, then performance by American students will rocket upwards.

Gates pumped $2 million into promoting the film, and also paid NBC to create a multi-day extravaganza called *Education Nation* to showcase its stars. Add in two episodes of Oprah, plus another of Larry King, and you had full-on media saturation.

But this visible assault was just the tip of the iceberg as Bill Gates, through the Gates Foundation, was already engaged in the most far-reaching public policy campaign ever waged, with the objective of completely transforming every aspect of the educational system in America.

The Gates Foundation is the largest philanthropic organization in the world, with assets of more than $40 billion.[3] The Gates Foundation funds a wide range of activities to meet its policy goals in education – which is its top domestic priority. There were several core principles that guided these investments:

- Quantitative data – especially test scores – would allow the education system to measure success and failure for the first time.

- There needs to be market-style competition in education, both between schools and within them.

- Teacher unions and due process restrict the ability of managers to fire those who are ineffective, so both should be weakened or eliminated.

- Democratically elected school boards are often an obstacle to sustained reform.

To act on these core ideas, the Gates Foundation funds a host of activities and organizations. The Foundation supports:

- Research by various think tanks, resulting in reports that support Gates' views. These reports are used in education policy settings, and the authors are flown around the country to testify before lawmakers in support of favored reforms.

- Advocacy by "grassroots" groups willing to support the Gates agenda. There are dozens of such groups, which organize in various constituencies. For example, when a bill was brought up in the Indiana state legislature that would gut due process and seniority protections for educators, a Gates-funded group called *Teach Plus* provided teachers to testify in support at the state capital.[4]

- Sponsorship of media outlets, and programming to support the cause of Gates-style reform. This includes *Waiting for Superman* and *Education Nation*, but also extends to funding news outlets like PBS *Newshour* and *National Public Radio*. Even *Education Week*, which has hosted my blog for the past six years, receives significant funding from Gates.[5]

- Direct influence on the US Department of Education, through which the Gates Foundation has been able to leverage federal expenditures in education into line with Gates' priorities. After the placement of several high ranked Gates Foundation officials at the Department of Education in 2009,[6] the competitive grant program known as *Race to the Top* was born. The criteria for judging these applications was aligned with Gates' priorities, and the Gates Foundation provided assistance to states willing to sign a memorandum of understanding in support of the Common Core standards.[7]

- Grants for the implementation of reforms such as the Common Core standards by professional organizations like *ASCD* (formerly the Association for Supervision and Curriculum Development), the National Board for Professional Teaching Standards (NBPTS), and even teacher unions, which have received millions for this purpose. Such grants pay for active compliance with reforms, and rob these organizations of their ability to be independent or critical regarding them. The Gates Foundation has spent more than $200 million for the creation and promotion of the Common Core standards, distributed to scores of organizations.[8]

This sort of focused, agenda-driven advocacy is new to the field of education. There had been philanthropic investment in education in the past, and organizations such as the Annenberg and Ford Foundations had provided support for various projects and experimental approaches. But the Gates Foundation's approach was different. Their starting point was "we know what is broken and we know how to fix it." Every dollar that was spent was aligned with their agenda, and their agenda was clearly communicated.

The Gates Foundation explains its process to potential grantees:

A. We do not make grants outside our funding priorities. In general, we directly invite proposals by directly contacting organizations.

We collaborate with organizations to develop proposals that align with our strategic priorities and the organization's focus and capabilities. This is an interactive process, building on the strengths of both organizations to shape a well-crafted grant that will achieve the intended results.[9]

In some cases, organizations such as inBloom sprang from the earth and blossomed into multi-million dollar non-profits with Gates funding. Because the Gates Foundation's expenditures are so vast, it has created a whole sector of organizations dependent on these funds.

The Gates Foundation has created an unprecedented role for philanthropy as the central driver pushing forward public policy in education. It has allied with other corporate philanthropies, such as the Broad and Walton foundations, which have similar objectives. These philanthropies, and the wealthy individuals associated with them, have managed to drive forward policies in line with Gates' priorities at every level, from the federal level on down.

In their 2014 paper, *Testing Theories of American Politics: Elites, Interest Groups, and Average Citizens*, Gilens and Page state:

The central point that emerges from our research is that economic elites and organized groups representing business interests have substantial independent impacts on U.S. government policy, while mass-based interest groups and average citizens have little or no independent influence.[10]

The Gates Foundation has used focused, agenda driven philanthropy to achieve the policy objectives of one of the world's wealthiest men. This is truly an oligarchy in action.

In the following chapters of this book, the actions of Bill Gates and his foundation related to education in America have been subjected to an extended critique from the perspective of a classroom teacher. The result is a thorough examination of the ideas and methods of the billionaire and his proxies that raises fundamental questions about the direction in which our education system has been led, the role of philanthropy, and the state of the 21st century American oligarchy.

Innovation in education is not destined to arrive from outside our schools, when all is standardized within. Innovation has always come from the creative spirit of students and teachers given the autonomy they need to experiment and be different.

Great nations rise and recede, and so does the power of the mighty.

The power that depends on spending billions of dollars to buy influence, and on the use of governmental coercion, is illusory. It exists only so long as the billions keep flowing, and the governmental power holds sway. The power of human imagination and desire for autonomy will always survive, and when the time is ripe, the mighty will fall.

Anthony Cody

June 8, 2014

Part I

The Assault on Public Education by Bill Gates

We're trying to start a movement. A movement started by you. A movement you're leading.

Irvin Scott, *Gates Foundation*[11]

It took some time for educators to grasp the transformation that was under way – and understanding the role of the Gates Foundation has taken time as well. But when we look back on the past six years or so, the outline becomes clear. Bill Gates has used his wealth to purchase every moving part of the educational system, and is using hundreds of different levers to move his agenda forward.

Chapter 1

Bill Gates' Big Play: How Much Can Money Buy in Education?

What would happen if one of the wealthiest men in the world decided to remake the institution of public education in America? What if that man believed he understood the secrets of success, and sought to align the nation's schools to his vision and methods? What if he decided to devote all his time and considerable money to this objective? Could he succeed? We are in the process of finding out just how far money and a sharply defined agenda can take you.

Bill Gates' first challenge was to define a vision. After offering grants to school districts to promote the breaking up of large schools into smaller ones, he discovered that this approach did not lead to consistently higher student performance. So he stepped back and said, OK, let's figure out just what IS going to increase those test scores? This was the crucial decision he made that has determined all other steps that have followed:

The purpose of schooling will be determined by the measurement that tells us if we have succeeded.

Although Bill Gates would perceive this as a neutral objective, in fact it has created a driving agenda for school change. The agenda is this: to re-craft the system so that it is just as relentlessly focused on test score improvement as any business is focused on making money.

How does one go about making your own agenda everyone else's?

Bill Gates had a huge head start, in that *No Child Left Behind (NCLB)* had already set the wheels in motion. The idea that test scores are all that matter was already encoded into federal law and funding policies. The trouble is that the *NCLB* law is punitive, cumbersome, illogical and bound to fail, by its own set of indicators. So we had to move beyond *NCLB*, and create a sustainable trajectory for test-driven reforms. This has been done in several ways. First, acknowledge that current tests are of limited value. We cannot abandon them because they are all we have, and we cannot ignore the data they give us, even though it is not all we might wish for. Develop a plan for a new generation of tests that will be clearly superior to existing tests. These new tests will be richer, incorporate technology, and will be based on new quasi-national standards that are likewise superior. The Gates Foundation has been a huge supporter of the Common Core Standards, and is partnering with the Pearson Foundation[12] to develop online reading and math courses aligned with the standards.

It can't hurt to have your high-level staff transfer over to working for the US Department of Education. And if lobbying rules would block this due to ethical considerations, simply get waivers.[13]

In October, 2011, Bill and Melinda Gates asserted:

It may surprise you--it was certainly surprising to us--but the field of education doesn't know very much at all about effective teaching.[14]

It did surprise me, because I am familiar with the amazing work done over the past two decades by educators who created the National Board for Professional Teaching Standards. The National Board defined the highest level of teaching[15] in line with all the things we value in a classroom. The standards include creating a strong classroom community that nurtures and supports all students. They include how well we meet the diverse needs of students from different cultures and linguistic backgrounds. The portfolios that teachers assemble need to provide strong evidence that students are learning, including work samples that show how the teacher has challenged and guided the student. In 2011 we saw that the National Board facing tremendous pressure to include test score data as an important indicator of teacher quality.[16]

Gates' approach to reforming the US education system to fit his vision has four key components:

First, research can lead the way:

The Gates Foundation is going after its goals by investing in research that implicitly defines the "effectiveness" of the education system as the ability to increase test scores. The studies have been in the works for years, and are now being released one after another. The way the research questions are posed, and the data is interpreted, allows you to control a great deal of the debate. For example, a November, 2011 study of charter schools came out, funded by the Gates Foundation, in which the key question posed focused on the "impact...on student outcomes," as measured by test scores.[17] Similarly, a huge project called *Measures of Effective Teaching*[18] appears to define effectiveness primarily by looking at test score gains.

Second, since the accountability devices in NCLB were clumsy and punitive, invent a host of new mechanisms to reward success as well as punish failure:

As much as possible, target these interventions down to the level of the individual teacher and student, to ensure compliance. Redefine professionalism for teachers so that it no longer means you have autonomy and responsibility for your work. Instead, being professional means you get paid for your results, and are subject to termination if you fail to help your students achieve what the predictive models project they ought to. Since teachers have been firmly opposed to this, do not make test scores the only means by which their performance is measured. Call this one of "multiple measures." But make sure other elements that are measured also align with test scores.

Third, get non-profit advocacy groups on your side:

If you hand out multi-million dollar grants to organizations that are piecing together their existence on much smaller sources, all of a sudden you can become their biggest sponsor. Pump money into advocacy groups like *Teach Plus*[19] and discover they are willing to lobby on behalf of things you value.

Fourth, influence the media:

Sponsor coverage of education in the media, including major television news events such as NBC's *Education Nation*, which, in 2010 was tied into the release of *Waiting For Superman*, which had a $2 million publicity effort sponsored by the Gates Foundation. This sponsorship will earn you prominent placement and glowing comments from the news hosts, such as during the 2011 *Education Nation Teacher Town Hall*, when Brian Williams said:

> The Gates Foundation, one of the sponsors of this event, and the largest single funder of education anywhere in the world. ***It's their facts that we're going to be referring to often to help along our conversation*** [emphasis added].[20]

This shows how media sponsorship and research can fit together to define the very facts that are discussed in the public arena. These definitions are rarely challenged, as they are the implicit conditions one must accept in order to gain sponsorship. This influence is rarely even acknowledged or discussed critically, such is its power and pervasiveness.

Chapter 2

Circular Reasoning at the Gates: Education Nation Off to a Confusing Start

In September 2010, NBC brought us the first *Education Nation*, developed in coordination with the release of the pro-charter school documentary, *Waiting For Superman*.[21] The network ran into a few bumps in the road, catching flak when it was pointed out[22] that panels were loaded with "superheroes" like Michelle Rhee, and that critical voices like Diane Ravitch, and those of classroom teachers, were largely absent.

In 2011, NBC made an effort to be a bit more balanced and inclusive of teachers voices, and the *Teacher Town Hall* program made a start in that direction. The comments from the teachers present were worth a listen, but my mind kept dwelling on the interview with Melinda Gates which opened the session. First, here are some of the things Brian Williams said about Melinda Gates and her husband.[23]

At the top of the show, we were told:

We're also going to be joined by Melinda Gates, co-chair of the Bill and Melinda Gates Foundation. Gates Foundation, one of the sponsors of this event, and the largest single funder of education anywhere in the world. It's their facts that we're going to be referring to often to help along our conversation.

Then, in his introduction of Melinda Gates, Brian Williams said:

You could refer to our guest as the top funder of education in the world. A partner and sponsor of this year's gathering. Also spending half a billion dollars to devise a way figure out what makes a great teacher, what makes them most effective. The estimates are the Gates Foundation has already spent, obviously a record for any education spending, spent or committed to spending five to seven billion dollars.

But I want to focus on what Melinda Gates said, because there is something deeply disturbing about the way the issues have been framed. And since this foundation is, according to Brian Williams, the source for the very facts that are guiding this conversation, it seems crucial to understand the thinking that is behind their work. Please review her thoughts, and see what you think of the reasoning that is at work. Brian Williams asks:

> You and your husband have always said this all comes back to a single relationship, a student and a teacher. What have you learned about what makes a great teacher?

Melinda Gates responds:

> Everybody says 'you can't just look at test scores at the end of the year, because there are so many factors, there's poverty and other things that go into this.' But nobody had done the research to say 'how do we know that a teacher's making a difference in a student's life?' So we set out to do this enormous piece of research. Three thousand teachers signed up in six different districts. We videoed the teachers, and we said 'at the end of the day, what is predictive of great teaching? What besides that test score?' And it turned out a teacher who is good one year is good usually in the second year. It turned out you could look at the test scores and see in terms of value added, how they had moved kids up in the system. But then you could also look at student perceptions. It turned out that student perceptions of a teacher were also predictive of how they would do at the end of the year and whether they learned all that material.

Brian Williams:

> How do you keep that from becoming a popularity contest?

Melinda Gates:

We learned you have to have multiple measures of what make a great teacher. Right now teachers are observed by their principals at regular intervals. We need to have peer observations. But we need to know that the tool that we're using -- there are ten different tools for peer observations. But which ones actually predict whether the students learned the material at the end of the year? So we need to test the peer observations, and the principal observations, and we need to look at the scores at the end of the year, and we need to look at the student data. When you ask the students did you have an effective teacher, you ask specific questions, 'did the teacher help you when you didn't understand the homework, or what you missed on your homework? Did they go help you learn that? Did the teacher get a sense of when he or she didn't explain the information well, and help get your class on track? Did your teacher manage the classroom well?' It turns out there are about six questions you can ask the students - not 'did you like the teacher,' but what they did in the classroom that actually measures and correlates to whether the test scores got better at the end of the year.

Do you notice what is bothering me? Melinda Gates begins by acknowledging that good teaching cannot be reduced to a test score - or at least that this is often said. She then asserts that the half billion dollars they have spent on research in this area have uncovered a number of things that can be measured that allow us to predict which teachers will have the highest test scores. A great teacher is defined over and over again as one who made sure students "learned the material at the end of the year."

If you look closely at how she describes peer observations, the method at work is even clearer. Teachers tend to support peer observation, because it can be a valuable basis for collaboration, which yields many benefits to us beyond possible test score gains. But what does Melinda Gates say about it? It can be worthwhile, BUT: only the models of peer observation that have been proven to raise test scores should be used. And presumably we can count on the Gates Foundation to provide us with that information.

In spite of all the billions they have spent, it appears that the Gates

Foundation is laboring under the same logical fallacy that doomed *No Child Left Behind*. In a way which employs circular reasoning, they have defined great teaching as that which results in the most gains on end of year tests, and then spent millions of dollars identifying indicators of teaching that will yield the best scores.

The most deceptive strategy is how they then try to pretend that these indicators are "multiple measures" of good teaching. In fact, these are simply indicators of teaching practices associated with higher test scores. In spite of Mrs. Gates' feint at the opening of her response, everything she describes, all these things that supposedly go beyond test scores - peer observations, student perceptions - are only deemed valid insofar as they are correlated with higher test scores.

Melinda Gates begins with the question "How do we know a teacher's making a difference in a student's life?" That is an excellent and complex question. However, when we look at her answer, we find she commits the logical fallacy known as "begging the question." The question she begs is "what defines great teaching?" This is not answered by finding teaching methods associated with higher test scores. This question remains hanging over the entire school reform enterprise. Until we answer that question, we are devising complex mechanisms to elevate test scores, assuming this will improve students' lives, when this is manifestly unproven. In fact, I would argue that many of the strategies used to boost scores are actually harmful to our students. And many dimensions of great teaching are not reflected in test scores -- and are systematically undermined when educators are held ever more "accountable" for these scores. This should remind us of the crucial need to teach critical thinking in our schools - and apply such thinking to the dilemmas we face.

The other thing that was rather disturbing was the omnipresence of the Gates Foundation's largesse. Towards the end of the show, Brian Williams offered this advice to viewers:

> This is a couple who have decided to give away their fortune. I heard two educators earlier today, one said to the other, "they never set out to do anything other than put money into education and help kids." So thanks to our audience for being mindful of that.

There was some pushback, however, and NBC deserves some credit for giving space for some differing views. New Haven teacher Matt Presser was one of the winners of an essay contest, and he offered his thoughts:

Too often school reform is something that is happening to our students as opposed to with them or for them, and so many decisions are being made by people in board rooms, people in the White House, when the real people who know what our students need are the people here today, the people in our classrooms every day.

This must have seemed to be a bit ungrateful to Brian Williams, because he then asked:

We just had Mrs. Gates here. This is a guy, I think the Forbes latest figure is $60 billion...here's the Gates family, spending upwards of $7 billion so far, haven't broken a sweat yet, trying to talk to you guys, ask you questions, including students, asking questions about what's working, what's not working. Do you support their efforts? Do you think it's money well spent?

Matt Presser replied:

I think it's a shame that we have to rely on philanthropy to support our schools, to make up for an educational debt that has accrued for generations. I think certain communities, especially in urban areas, have been neglected by education for so many years, we have so much to make up for - not just in education, but in housing policy and job discrimination. In so many areas across the country, that even those efforts to get more money into our schools, there needs to be more a holistic approach, instead of just something that is thrown at our schools.

But perhaps the most potent counterweight to the Gates approach was offered by teacher John Hunter. He said:

My first job interview, I asked the supervisor, what should I do? She said 'What do you want to do?' As a teacher, to be given that kind of open space, that kind of mandate-less position to be in where you can create out of the emptiness, it allowed me to create that kind of template for my students, where I could ask them, 'what would

YOU like to do today? What is your passion? What drives you?' If the students have the interest and you build towards that, then they can come with more passion for learning.

He took advantage of this latitude to create a now-famous eight-week long interactive game[24] where his students are challenged to solve world problems. Was this great teaching? Do we have to wait until we see how his students performed on the end-of-year standardized tests to find out?

Chapter 3

Teachers Face Good Cops or Bad Cops in Push for Evaluations

In the spring of 2012, newspaper readers saw something strange. Both Bill Gates and Michelle Rhee took to editorial pages to criticize the publication of teacher ratings in newspapers, suggesting that these scores alone do not give a full picture of teacher performance. What we have here seems to be a classic case of good cop/bad cop, where Rupert Murdoch's *New York Post* plays the abusive bad cop, publishing the names of teachers, and singling out the city's "worst" teachers[25] for public humiliation. And Gates, Rhee and the Department of Education ride to the rescue, offering the sweeter, but nonetheless damaging "multiple measures" evaluation models.

In parallel with Rhee's missive, Bill Gates wrote an opinion piece in the New York Times that said:

Value-added ratings are one important piece of a complete personnel system. But student test scores alone aren't a sensitive enough measure to gauge effective teaching, nor are they diagnostic enough to identify areas of improvement. Teaching is multifaceted, complex work. A reliable evaluation system must incorporate other measures of effectiveness, like students' feedback about their teachers and classroom observations by highly trained peer evaluators and principals.[26]

Here we have the good cop's case for "multiple measures," very neatly made against a counterpoint, the bad cop's use of test scores only.

But there is a big problem that remains. The evaluation model we are being offered is driven by several false assumptions.

False Assumption One:

Schools in our nation are saddled with a significant number of crummy teachers, and achievement will rise dramatically if we can bring in new evaluation systems to reliably identify and weed out these teachers. Bill Gates, appearing on Oprah in 2010, asserted that if only we could get rid of the bad teachers, our schools would shoot from the bottom of international rankings to the top.[27]

It is time to recognize that our international standings have become a meaningless exercise in political grandstanding, with little attention to the underlying data they are drawn from.[28] Second, the idea that we can fire teachers on our way to better schools has a fatal flaw. It assumes there are fresh teachers ready to take the place of those we fire. Given that our high poverty schools already have teacher turnover rates in the neighborhood of 20% a year, and about 50% of beginning teachers wash out in their first five years, the idea that we will improve our schools by firing even more is hard to believe. Where are the high quality teachers going to come from to replace those we fire? School improvement is much more complex than this, and its foundation has to be based on building the profession.

False Assumption Two:

Test scores, and a host of secondary indicators found to be correlated with higher test scores, are the means by which we determine teacher quality. This takes a very keen eye to detect, because Bill Gates and the researchers he sponsors are not fools. They know that test scores have been somewhat discredited as a result of *NCLB*'s single-minded focus on them. But the sophisticated measures that Gates offers are, unfortunately, mostly tied back to test scores. And what about those student surveys he mentions? As Melinda Gates explained last fall, the questions were checked to see which ones correlate with higher student test scores (see chapter 2). The training that the peer observers and principals get can make sure they are watching for teacher behaviors associated with better student achievement, i.e. higher test scores.

If you visit the *Measures of Effective Teaching (MET)* project,[29] which is the flagship of the Gates Foundation's work in this arena, you find that teacher quality is defined in terms of the ability of a teacher to produce gains in student achievement. Then the project seeks different ways to measure this ability. There is the direct measurement - the scores. And then there are a host of other indicators - observations, student surveys and so on. But the core idea of teacher "effectiveness" is tied to the "effect", which is defined as student achievement. And student achievement is always defined by some sort of test performance.

False Assumption Three:

Teacher quality will increase with detailed and specific feedback. This *would* be true, if we had a solid working definition of the qualities we are after. Unfortunately, we are working with a circular definition of that equates teacher quality with the ability to raise student performance on tests, and then seeks to reinforce teacher behaviors associated with this ability.

What we need to build strong teachers are more diverse indicators of student learning. As Rog Lucido explained,[30] student learning cannot be adequately reflected by a score, or even by a set of scores using multiple measures. Student learning can be described, and it can be exemplified, through the use of authentic evidence such as student writing, projects, presentations, research and other products. We need to work with a much richer set of student outcomes than we get by simply focusing on student achievement as it is currently defined. And we will not get there by the circular methods being promoted by the Gates Foundation and the US Department of Education.

Is there an appropriate use for test score data in teacher evaluations? Absolutely! In the report, *A Quality Teacher in Every Classroom*,[31] which was issued back in 2010 by *Accomplished California Teachers*, we took a close look at all the possible sources of information that might be brought to bear in a high quality teacher evaluation process. We wrote:

> They should be evaluated with tools that assess professional standards of practice in the classroom, augmented with evidence of student outcomes. Beyond standardized test scores, those outcomes should

include performance on authentic tasks that demonstrate learning of content; presentation of evidence from formative classroom assessments that show patterns of student improvement; the development of habits that lead to improved academic success (personal responsibility, homework completion, willingness and ability to revise work to meet standards), along with contributing indicators like attendance, enrollment and success in advanced courses, graduation rates, pursuit of higher education, and work place success.

In practice, this means we should oppose the formulaic use of a "Value Added Model (VAM)", which research has shown to be highly unstable at the level of individual teachers. This method should not be used for any significant part of an evaluation, even if other measures are included. It is simply not ready for prime time. Of course, we must also oppose the publication of teacher ratings based on these models. If you are reading this and thinking "How much harm could it do to use these ratings as one of several indicators of teacher quality?" please take a look at Gary Rubinstein's analysis of the New York City VAM data.[32]

This data is garbage, and it has no business being any part of a professional teacher's evaluation. The "Early Findings" of the *MET Project* exploring teacher evaluation brings us the good cop/bad cop dichotomy quite clearly:

> The public discussion usually portrays only two options: the status quo (where there is no meaningful feedback for teachers) and a seemingly extreme world in which tests scores alone determine a teacher's fate. Our results suggest that's a false choice. It is possible to combine measures from different sources to get a more complete picture of teaching practice. The measures should allow a school leader to both discern a teacher's ability to produce results and offer specific diagnostic feedback. Value-added scores alone, while important, do not recommend specific ways for teachers to improve.[33]

So here we have it, teachers. You can be pilloried in public based on test scores alone, or you can have the magic fairy dust of multiple measures to soften the blows. We can do this the easy way, or the hard way. How do you want it?

Chapter 4

Cui Bono? The Question Rarely Asked, Let Alone Investigated

As our public schools are systematically re-engineered for dubious reasons, with questionable results, by people of uncertain motives, there is a disturbing lack of skepticism on the part of our watchdogs for the public good, journalists. One of the basic principles of reporting is to ask "cui bono" - who benefits? In the Watergate scandal, the key informant whispered to reporters Woodward and Bernstein, "Follow the money." But very few reporters today seem to be "following the money" in the field of education.

Veteran education reporter John Merrow delved into cheating scandals on his blog, *Taking Note*:

> In other words, we're cheating kids on their tests and stealing essential courses like art and music from them! Add to that, we are lying -- because when kids get phony scores telling them they are proficient when they need help, that's an out-and-out lie. At what point does this trifecta -- lying, cheating and stealing -- become a felony? Seriously!

> In the face of this disheartening news, one has to ask, "who benefits?" I'm stumped. Certainly not children, parents and teachers. Could it be the testing companies? Perhaps it's the bevy of expert 'consultants' who advise school systems on how to raise test scores, how to calculate the 'value added' that individual teachers provide, and how to make education more 'businesslike' and efficient?

A far more important question than 'who benefits?' is: What are we going to do about it?[34]

I want to make a special plea to John Merrow and other journalists. Reporters hold a sacred public trust and fill a role no one else in society can. Before the rest of the public is even aware that something ought to be done, they must be informed that there is a problem. We need some real reporting here. And that means taking some risks.

We have had a very heavy push from a host of sources to convince us all that "reform" of a certain sort is required in our schools. These are the false ideas we are up against:

Our public schools are failing: Establishing this is essential because it justifies their destruction - and replacement by far more profitable ventures. There is ample evidence this is not so.

Charter schools are far more efficient than public schools, and produce better results as well: A 2012 report contradicts the first claim,[35] and the largest study of charters ever conducted contradicts the second.[36] But many stories about charters do not dig for these facts.

The problems associated with standardized tests will be solved with technical innovations and the new Common Core standards: Narrowing of the curriculum will be fixed by having more tests in more subjects. Critical thinking will be fostered by better standards and tests scored by computers. Research on this is hard to find - these are largely the promises made by those who are selling these solutions. But the unproven assumption that these things are so underlies many stories now coming out about the Common Core.

Teachers are the number one reason students are doing poorly, and thus if we can eliminate the ineffective ones, performance will shoot through the roof: This has spawned a host of reforms, including the elimination of due process, and VAM systems to evaluate teachers using their test scores. Media outlets have actively propagated these unreliable methods. The *Los Angeles Times* created its own VAM system and published teacher ratings in 2011,[37] and in 2012 New York newspapers published teacher ratings and wrote exposes of the "worst teachers" based on them.[38]

When we look closely at each aspect of this narrative, we can see who stands to benefit - and often they are the same people and organizations promoting their self-serving solutions. The "who benefits?" question is key, because until it is confronted, we will have no idea what must be done. So let's take a look at "who benefits?" starting with those mentioned by John Merrow.

Testing companies: Yes, clearly. They are already reaping huge rewards from the expansion of testing over the past decade. And with the Common Core standards we are going to see an even greater expansion in the number and frequency of tests, and the courses which will be tested.

Those calculating the 'value added' that individual teachers provide: William Sanders[39] began as an agricultural economist, and then applied these methods to measuring the impact that individual teachers make on student performance. Today, districts can purchase from him a complex system that can be used to rate their teachers.

Curriculum designers/publishers: Those creating curriculum aligned with the new Common Core Standards. As Secretary Arne Duncan's chief of staff Joanne Weiss pointed out in 2011:

> The development of common standards and shared assessments radically alters the market for innovation in curriculum development, professional development, and formative assessments. Previously, these markets operated on a state-by-state basis, and often on a district-by-district basis. But the adoption of common standards and shared assessments means that education entrepreneurs will enjoy national markets where the best products can be taken to scale.[40]

Consultants who advise schools on how to raise test scores: There has been a proliferation of organizations who guarantee results, attacking this issue from every possible angle. We have specialists in literacy, math, and school turnarounds. We have after-school test preparation[41] and course-embedded test preparation.[42]

But let's dig a bit deeper -- because the list of those who are benefiting is long, and is a major reason why this juggernaut has proved so hard to halt. Here are a few more to add to John Merrow's short list:

Charter school operators: Some of whom have been indicted recently.[43]

Teacher Leaders and organizations: Like ASCD,[44] who are now promoting themselves as experts capable of doing the professional development needed to allow teachers to succeed with the Common Core.

Alternative Credentialing/Leadership programs: Such as *Teach for America (TFA)* and *The NewTeacher Project (TNTP)*, who get large grants both from the government and from philanthropies based on their willingness to replace experienced teachers with short term novices, in spite of their high turnover rates. Huge recent grants in excess of $100 million have made expansion the number one priority for *TFA*, so as a result, the organization is moving into areas that do not have any teacher shortages at all. *TFA* got on board the standardized testing bandwagon years ago, and *TNTP* authored the report, The Widget Effect,[45] that prompted the current drive to revamp teacher evaluations incorporating test scores, in order to get rid of "ineffective teachers."

Astroturf groups: Such as *Teach Plus* who, with generous grant funding, develop what appear to be grassroots advocates for "reform" proposals such as Senate Bill 1 in Indiana,[46] which tied teacher pay and evaluations to test scores. The school "reform" super group, *StudentsFirstNY* and its Michelle Rhee/Joel Klein led predecessor *Education Reform Now* poured more than $10 million[47] into lobbying to influence lawmakers in New York.

Technology and software companies: Many of the assessments and curriculum systems associated with the Common Core rely on computers to deliver instruction and to test student learning. This means a huge expansion both in hardware and software, and an enormous shift of scarce education dollars into technology and away from human beings working with students. Just watch as this is being spun as "efficiency," as in the *Rocketship* schools, which have greatly expanded class size and cut the number of teachers, as they have students learning on computers two hours a day.[48]

Virtual Schools: Along the same lines, these "schools" are being granted licenses, and are even succeeding, with the help of the *American*

Legislative Exchange Council (ALEC) in getting laws passed[49] that mandate that students take some courses online.

There is also a big overlap - some of the same businesses profiting from tests will also sell services to save your schools when they are failing.[50] There is big money being made -- one big test publisher, Pearson, reported US sales of its products totaled $4.8 billion for the year 2013.[51]

Corporate/philanthropic synergy at work was showcased in 2011 when the Gates and Pearson Foundations announced[52] a partnership aimed at crafting complete, online curricula for those standards in mathematics and English/language arts that span nearly every year of a child's pre-collegiate education.

There is a further overlap with the realm of journalism itself, which might be part of the reason the question of "who benefits" is so rarely investigated. Media titan Rupert Murdoch owns the education technology company Amplify, and has made no bones about his aims:

> When it comes to K through 12 education, we see a $500 billion sector in the US alone that is waiting desperately to be transformed by big breakthroughs that extend the reach of great teaching.[53]

And those of us, myself included, who work in journalism supported by education industry advertising and foundation grants, also are affected. *Education Week*[54] and *Learning Matters*,[55] the non-profit headed by John Merrow, both are in this category.

To their credit, *Education Week* never attempted to stifle my perspective. I hope John Merrow enjoys a similar sense of independence, and look forward to following his investigations in this rich journalistic vein. If he really starts looking, he should not remain stumped for long. He would be a rare element, a mainstream journalist with the guts to buck the dominant narrative and reveal the uncomfortable truth about the path we have taken, and the decidedly mixed motives[56] of those leading us there. He would join some other brave reporters, Valerie Strauss and Lyndsey Layton at the *Washington Post*, Stephanie Simon of Politico, Greg Toppo at *USA Today*, who have shown us it is possible.

I am not saying that every person or entity that stands to gain is some sort of craven creature controlled by avarice. Many have good intentions, and may be sincere in their ambitions to help students. However, as that great investigative reporter Upton Sinclair famously said, "It is difficult to get a man to understand something, when his salary depends upon his not understanding it."[57] Those of us in the tenuous world of 21st century journalism are not immune from this phenomenon.

When I have raised this concern in the past, it has been dismissed as a "conspiracy theory." A conspiracy is defined as a secret, usually illegal, plan concocted by several people. This is no conspiracy. It is not secret -- just largely ignored. And thanks to the machinations of *ALEC* and the cooperation of politicians from both parties, it is usually legal as well.

The fact that someone benefits does not mean their ideas should automatically be dismissed, but we should exercise a far greater degree of skepticism than we now see, and objective evidence should be sought before we accept as truth the latest self-serving demands for "courageous action," or proclamations of success. Real reporting means not just asking "cui bono?" but finding out and warning the public when their interests and institutions are threatened.

Chapter 5

Bill Gates Discovers Money Cannot Buy Teachers

The June 8, 2013 *Seattle Times* tells us of a strange problem encountered by the richest man in the world. He has discovered that his money is not working its magic in education -- teachers are not for sale.

The Gates Foundation has spent the past decade promoting hard-hitting reforms. Organizations they fund have conducted research, lobbied politicians, and advanced policies that have brought us VAM teacher and principal evaluations, charter school expansion, *Teach For America* corps members, and merit pay. They have poured millions into efforts to shape public opinion, sponsoring *Education Nation* and the propaganda documentary *Waiting for Superman*, and its star, Michelle Rhee. They have told us how important teachers are, but in spite of all this attention, teachers seem positively ungrateful.

So now the Gates Foundation is on what has been called a "charm offensive." According to Seattle Times reporter Linda Shaw,[58] in February, 2012 the Gates Foundation brought 250 teachers to a hotel in Arizona to share their new vision. The Gates Foundation's Irvin Scott said, "We're trying to start a movement. A movement started by you. A movement you're leading."

Is this not a paradox worthy of Lewis Carroll?

Money tends to distort reality. Those who have it think that they can use it to get what they want. And those that have a lot, think they can get a lot. But when what you want to control is something as big as the way children are educated, and the conditions under which an entire profession is trained, supervised and paid, you are going to run into some bumps along the way.

Ultimately, there are three ways to get people to do something you want them to do. One is to force them, by making the consequences for not complying onerous or unacceptable. The second is to lure them, by offering some sort of bribe or incentive. The third is to get them excited about your ideas, whereupon they may engage with enthusiasm.

In my experience, real change in education only comes with the third of these methods, because the first two inspire more resistance than cooperation.

You may get people to buckle under and teach to the test because they fear being fired if their scores don't rise. You may get them to have Professional Learning Community (PLC) meetings focused on test data that supposedly allows them to "personalize" their instruction. But this sort of change does not go very deep or inspire much enthusiasm, because it is not rooted in our deepest aspirations for our students. And people sense when they are being manipulated and coerced - they resent it, and they resist. That is what the Gates Foundation is getting now - resentment and resistance. The sort of professional growth we need in our schools comes from a different, deeper source of inspiration. It is not the product of fear or desire for rewards. It is from that spirit of compassion and creativity that drew most of us into teaching in the first place.

So far, I have not seen any evidence that the Gates Foundation has learned this lesson. When I look at the substance of the editorials written by Gates and his representatives, I see an acknowledgement that some of the things they have pushed for may have gone too far. In the *Seattle Times* article, I am quoted as wanting Gates to apologize for all the destructive policies his money has inspired. I do want that, but much more important would be the recognition that we need a very different direction.

It might start with some curiosity. What do teachers who have not been "empowered" by the Gates Foundation's largesse think of their work? The comments to the June 8, 2013 *Seattle Times* article were rather scathing. One of the milder ones reads:

> If I could send Mr. Gates just one message, it would be this: Almost all teachers are proud of the progress of their students and enjoy sharing evidence of that progress with administrators, other teachers and parents. In California, I worked under the Stull Act for many years, which required me to prove student progress. To help with that, I kept a portfolio for every student in which I kept samples of student work, compositions and tests. I never resented doing this because ensuring student progress was my job. (I am now retired).
>
> What teachers are against is being evaluated on the basis of standardized test scores. The reasons for this should be obvious: these tests are not designed to differentiate between classroom and home learning; they are often not valid; they are not professionally administered or handled. In short, an excellent teacher could get mediocre test scores, while a poor teacher could get good ones. These test scores most often correlate closely with the socioeconomic background of the students and not with classroom instruction.
>
> If Mr. Gates continues to include teachers in his efforts to reform education, I believe he will find that the average teacher is NOT against being evaluated, as long as it is done fairly.

And another comment provides an avenue for even more feedback, should the Gates Foundation be interested. Several teachers have launched a new project, *Teachers' Letters to Bill Gates*, with a website,[59] a *Facebook* page,[60] and a *Twitter* account.[61] If teachers have any thoughts to share with the Gates Foundation, here is a place to do that.

The coercive strain of education reform advanced by the Gates Foundation has left them in a bad spot, if they want to start, or help lead any sort of movement of teachers in this country. So far, the minor course adjustments that have been made to the rhetoric surrounding reform have been insufficient to convince educators that the Gates Foundation has learned any meaningful lessons.

The key to understanding the way out may lie in the paradox offered by the Gates Foundation's Irvin Scott in 2012. Teachers are already leading their own movement, a movement they started themselves. The

Gates Foundation cannot start that movement, and they cannot succeed in "empowering" any leaders who may have aligned with their models of reform. The idea that teachers will be led by some movement started or sponsored by the Gates foundation must be discarded. Teachers, just like any group of people, have to choose their own leaders, and must be inspired from values held within.

We are engaged in some formative assessment here, and feedback is being offered. It remains to be seen if the Gates Foundation is open to new understandings.

Chapter 6

Bill Gates Goes to College Has He Learned From His K12 Project?

The new Big Man on Campus is none other than Bill Gates, who, having spent the past decade making K12 education more tightly measured and efficient, is now bringing his market-driven methods to higher education. Buckle up, boys and girls, it's gonna be a bumpy ride.

A July, 2013 analysis in the *Chronicle for Higher Education*[62] paints a picture which is by now familiar to public school educators. The declared goal here is the same as with public education. In the past decade, the Gates Foundation has put several hundred million dollars into efforts that have as their goal the reduction in poverty. For some unknown reason, actual poverty has sharply increased during this same decade. But let's not let that stop the project.

Just as with its K12 flagship effort, the Common Core, the Gates Foundation wants to transform higher education to insure a "competitive workforce." To that end, they would like college to be cheaper, more accessible, and more targeted towards the specific skills desired by employers. Instead of a broad education where a college student might take courses across a range of subjects, the new model has students demonstrating "competencies" by passing tests in specific areas, and receiving a certificate upon completion.

According to Gates:

The education we're currently providing, or the way we're providing it, just isn't sustainable... Instead we have to ask, 'How can we use technology as a tool to recreate the entire college experience? How can we provide a better education to more people for less money?'[63]

I have some major concerns about this.

First, is it a "better education" to have students taking courses online, seldom if ever interacting with professors or even fellow students?

We have already seen what "virtual education" looks like in the public school arena,[64] especially when coupled to the profit motive. The largest chain of virtual schools in the nation has shown very poor performance results. The highly promoted Massive Open Online Courses (MOOCs) have been marked by completion rates below ten percent,[65] recent studies have found.

It is possible that having students learn via online courses is more "efficient," but another recent study reported in *the Chronicle of Higher Education* also showed that this approach might widen the achievement gap:

The researchers examined 500,000 courses taken by more than 40,000 community and technical college students in Washington State. They found that students in demographic groups whose members typically struggle in traditional classrooms are finding their troubles exacerbated in online courses.

The study found that all students who take more online courses, no matter the demographic, are less likely to attain a degree. However, some groups--including black students, male students, younger students, and students with lower grade-point averages--are particularly susceptible to this pattern.[66]

Time Magazine shared a similar warning a year ago:

In terms of learning on the college level, the Department of Education looked at thousands of research studies from 1996 to 2008 and found that in higher education, students rarely learned as much from online courses as they did in traditional classes. In fact, the report found that the biggest benefit of online instruction came from a blended learning environment that combined technology with traditional methods, but warned that the uptick had more to do with the increased amount of individualized instruction students got in that environment, not the presence of technology. For all but the brightest, the more time students spend with traditional instruction, the better they seem to do.[67]

Second, is there any evidence that middle class jobs await this new generation of "certificated" graduates?

Unfortunately not much. According to this report from the US Bureau of Labor Statistics,[68] looking forward to 2018, only 23% of all job openings require a bachelor's degree or more. About 67% require a high school degree OR LESS. Increasing the number of people with college degrees (or "certificates of competency") may make employers happy. But given that there is little evidence of a shortage of skilled workers,[69] an increase in their number is only likely to push wages downward.

Third, is education simply job preparation? Have colleges abdicated any role in engaging students in bigger questions? Or any real questions at all?

Stepping beyond the purely economic realm, we must examine our purpose for educating young people in the first place. Our colleges and universities certainly have a role in the national economy, and a college education may prepare students for the world of work, through some combination of the discipline of study, habits of mind, and specific knowledge required for any given field. But education - even K12 education - ought to be much more than this.

Fourth, a measurement-driven system reduces everything to that which can easily be measured.

In contrast to this approach, as a science teacher, I see education as a series of learner-driven inquiries. Our students should be given invitations and opportunities to investigate the world they are inheriting. We are delivering them into an unholy mess, and just as previous generations have done, they need to reshape the world. That means they ought to be active learners, exploring and questioning. Education should not be reduced to passing a series of tests so some unseen authority can "certify" your competence for the benefit of some employer who may or may not need you.

Gates' suggestion that we must flatten expenditures on education is unwarranted.[70] We have the most productive economy in the world. The money that corporations avoided paying in taxes in 2012 could have covered the entire 2013 Federal education budget.[71]

This report, "*Why Our Schools Are Broke*," reveals that:

For 2011 and 2012, the 155 companies paid just 1.8 percent of their total income in state taxes, and 3.6 percent of their declared U.S. income. The average required rate for the 50 states is 6.56 percent.[72]

These unpaid taxes are more than all K12 education budget cuts combined. And corporate profits are at an all-time high,[73] while wages continue to fall.

But whether at the K12 level or in higher education, schools are facing the same push from Gates and his allies in business. Schools must serve employers, and must do it more cheaply than ever.

I entered teaching to serve my students. I think they will be best equipped by experiencing the discipline of learning, of inquiry and exploration. I hope those that go to college get to learn about lots of things, and engage with exciting and challenging professors and classmates. The push for efficiency will yield short-term profits, but in the long run our students, and our economy, will suffer.

Those who are serious about fighting poverty might want to be more direct about it. How about an increase in the minimum wage? Take a look at Australia, where the minimum wage is far more than it is in the US.[74] How about corporations paying their taxes so we have the funds needed for our schools? How about ending the drug war, and reducing the number of Americans behind bars?

The Gates Foundation suggested they wanted to learn from their experiences in K12 education before seeking to transform higher education. Those of us who have experienced their involvement in K12 education might suggest they wait a little longer, and learn a little more, before they graduate and begin their work in higher education.

Chapter 7

Is ASCD Embracing Market-Driven Education Reform?

Another day, another headline on ASCD's *Smartbrief* email newsletter[75] extolling some new Common Core strategy. ASCD signed on as an early endorser of Common Core,[76] and in 2011, the Gates Foundation awarded ASCD a grant of $3 million "to provide teachers and school leaders with supports to implement the Common Core State Standards at the district, school, and classroom levels."[77] In July of 2013, ASCD won an additional $244,000, "to support implementation of the Common Core State Standards."[78]

I have generally positive feelings towards ASCD. I recall in 2010, when ASCD president Gene Carter wrote a public letter in response to Oprah's show on *Waiting for Superman*. He wrote:

> As a career educator and the executive director of ASCD, an education association of 160,000 educators worldwide, I was dismayed that your show on education reform excluded a key demographic from the dialogue: teachers. Yet the research---and your high-profile guests---say a child's teacher is the most important factor to determining his or her success.

> Moreover, simplistically dividing a profession of 5 million people into 'good teachers' and 'bad teachers' misses an important opportunity to show how all educators must continue to learn, develop, and grow throughout their careers.[79]

In the more distant past, *Educational Leadership*, ASCD's journal, carried articles detailing the problems with the high stakes testing paradigm.[80] And *Educational Leadership* continues to feature strong explorations of issues like teacher evaluation and professional development, including an article I contributed recently on the subject of teacher leadership.[81]

ASCD's coverage of the controversies regarding Common Core has been a bit less balanced. Their *Common Core State Standards Myths and Facts*[82] perpetuates the idea that state adoption of the standards was "voluntary" when we all know adoption has been the result of a combination of *Race to the Top* carrots and *NCLB* waiver sticks. The article presents a host of other glowing promises about Common Core that neither ASCD nor anyone else can deliver upon.

Educational Leadership has treated the controversy over Common Core literacy instruction in a one-sided fashion, by presenting this article by Timothy Shanahan, derisively titled *The Common Core Ate My Baby and Other Urban Legends*.[83] There are many respected literacy experts who strongly disagree with his stance, but their views were not shared, except to be dismissed by him as nonsense. The same journal has also published articles expressing skepticism such as this one by Tom Loveless, *The Common Core Initiative: What are the Chances of Success*.[84] But the thrust of the journal and work of ASCD has become dominated by the push to implement Common Core.

I was also a bit stunned when I saw the program for ASCD's 2014 *Leadership Institute for Legislative Action*, and their choice for this year's keynote speaker; Rick Hess of the *American Enterprise Institute*.[85]

This raises some questions for me as to the direction the ASCD is taking in its legislative advocacy. This is not to slight Rick Hess. He writes a thought-provoking blog at *Education Week*,[86] and often has interesting things to say. But he represents the *American Enterprise Institute*, and is a strong advocate of market-based reform. In 2013 Hess wrote about the conservative school board in Douglas County, Colorado, describing the place as "the most interesting school district in America." He wrote:

The district's distinctive aim of going from good to great, rather than from poor to passable, is remarkable in the annals of contemporary school reform. For Douglas County, school choice is not seen not as a "ticket out" of failing schools, but a way to encourage customization and to offer more paths for students to choose.[87]

It came out (and Hess subsequently acknowledged in his blog) that Hess had been paid a substantial fee for consulting with the district he was praising. This article from *Our Castle Rock News* reveals how much the District got for their money:

AEI's Rick Hess and Max Eden wrote a paper, "The Most Interesting School District in America," that the district emailed to parents Sept. 18 as a "just-released white paper" and did not identify as a district-paid product.

The Feb. 6, 2013, contract between DCSD and AEI outlines a $30,000 payment and scope of services, asking the organization to "research, create, publish and publicize" a 25-30 page white paper with three to five sidebars. DCSD's requirements for the paper included a description of the district, the problems its reforms are meant to address, how the reforms are "new and different," district challenges in the face of its reforms and lessons learned. The district's lead spokeswoman and its foundation director, Cinamon Watson, signed as DCSD's representative.

Hess and Watson also exchanged emails about the paper in which the writer asked for further guidance.

"Ideally, we would love for you all to help us help you," Hess wrote in a March 22 email to Watson. "Rather, we would prefer it if you would tell us what you want us to focus on, what is most worthy of attention, what you'd like to see written about, and what your general angle on it and the paper is."[88]

Remember, this paper was commissioned and released in the context of a contentious election in which conservative "reformers" were challenged by candidates less supportive of vouchers and other market-based reforms. Apparently this is the way the free market works in education policy writing.

When I tweeted a question, asking if the choice of Hess as a keynote speaker reflected an embrace of free market education reform, ASCD responded: "Hosting speakers isn't endorsement of their positions. ASCD strives to provide members with diverse viewpoints & opinions." This response is supported by the fact that the speaker at the previous year's event was Diane Ravitch, who no doubt delivered a very different message to the group. I spoke with David Griffith, ASCD's Director of Public Policy, and he said:

> We are supporters of public education. Just because we have someone speak does not mean we agree with them. Hess is a compelling speaker, and has provocative things to say. There is a privatization movement, so it behooves us to hear from them. Conference participants will be visiting Capitol Hill, and the House is controlled by Republicans. It is not that we're supporting one view or another, we want them be prepared and understand what the arguments are around this.

ASCD is free to invite whomever they wish to speak to their organization, but at this moment in history, when the future of public education hangs in the balance, the choice of an outspoken advocate of privatization is a bit disturbing.

Taking a look at the actual 2013 policy agenda of ASCD,[89] there is likewise reason for concern. The document says that the organization will be advocating:

> **Support meaningful accountability systems** - Any comprehensive determination of student proficiency, school quality, or educator effectiveness must take into account student growth, use multiple measures of evaluation beyond standardized test scores, and differentiate among levels of performance.

We are seeing how this "multiple measures" language translates into practice. As much as 50% of a teacher's evaluation may be based on highly unstable "value added" (VAM) scores drawn from standardized tests. Evaluations go "beyond" this, by including administrator observations. And did we mention - the administrator's evaluations are likewise required to include test scores?

Everyone - even Michelle Rhee[90] - will use this "multiple measures" language, to distance himself or herself from a straw man they are implicitly creating - an evaluation system based ONLY on test scores. Such systems have never existed, so far as I know. But you do not have to make test scores 100% of an evaluation scheme to make them hugely consequential.

Common Core is illuminating the way our democratic processes have been systematically bypassed by the combined efforts of big philanthropies and the federal government. *Race to the Top* was used to get state officials to sign on to Common Core with little discussion, and apparently professional organizations such as ASCD have simply accepted this as a fait accompli, forgoing any responsibility for real debate.

Organizations like ASCD are being directly paid to "support implementation" of Common Core, which in effect converts them into advocates for the controversial standards. These organizations are also directly benefitting from the bonanza associated with professional development and curriculum made necessary by the shift to the Common Core standards. Is the organization capable of taking an independent stance, once it has accepted grants such as these?

The ASCD's Legislative agenda is silent on the issue of privatization of public education, or on the expansion of vouchers. It is silent on the spread of low-quality virtual charter schools. It is silent about the expansion of testing that is coming with the new Common Core tests, or the diversion of billions of education dollars into technology these tests will require.

I have perhaps a fanciful vision of what professional organizations like ASCD should be. In the absence of genuine public debate[91] about the adoption of the Common Core, I wish that our professional organizations would create space for that debate to occur. Of course that is hard to do once you have accepted millions of dollars to promote the project!

As the very institution of public education is threatened by the push to privatize, I wish that ASCD would provide some real debate over this trend, and the effects of market-driven systems on public schools. I would like to see organizations like ASCD step forward as advocates for policies that serve all children, and against the transformation of schools into profit centers. But choosing a keynote speaker from the American

Enterprise Institute will not help to deliver this debate.

As we step forward into implementation of Common Core tests, I think it is the absolute responsibility of leaders of organizations like ASCD, who have the expertise to understand the terrible effects that high stakes tests have on children, to take a clear and public stand against the consequences attached to them. That includes their use as one of the "multiple measures" of teacher performance, and as justification for the closing of low-scoring schools. Otherwise the transition to Common Core will have accomplished one of its tacit goals - the conversion of critics of *NCLB* into backhanded promoters of the next generation of high stakes tests.

Chapter 8

Is Gates Money Going to Influence the National Board?

A billionaire by the name of Tom Perkins recently made headlines with his suggestion that since people like him pay more taxes; they ought to have more political power. His idea to make things more fair? "You don't get to vote unless you pay $1 in taxes... If you pay $1 million in taxes, you get a million votes."[92]

Of course other billionaires figured out long ago that there are other ways to gain political control over democratic processes. You do not need direct control over votes if you can access other levers of power. Our education system is in the process of being transformed, and the biggest billionaire in the nation has led the charge for the past decade. But Bill Gates' project has run into a few bumps in the road recently, so once again he and his wife Melinda have been on the hustings, doing their best to convince us that all is well.

Bill Gates offered a column in *USA Today* in February 2014, commending the Common Core.[93] In the pretense of debunking myths, Gates promotes falsehoods, such as the assertion that teachers, parents and students participated in the creation of the standards. Creation refers to the origin, the genesis of something. In that regard, we can enter the *Wayback Machine* to discover that no, teachers were not involved in the drafting of the standards.[94] But he really goes into the realm of myth-making when he states this:

These are standards, just like the ones schools have always had; they are not a curriculum. They are a blueprint of what students need to know, but they have nothing to say about how teachers teach that information. It's still up to local educators to select the curriculum.

In fact, the standards will give teachers more choices. When every state had its own standards, innovators making new educational software or cutting-edge lesson plans had to make many versions to reach all students. Now, consistent standards will allow more competition and innovation to help teachers do their best work.

An earlier statement by Gates was far more frank regarding his hopes for the Common Core. In 2009, he said "Identifying Common Standards is just the starting point. We'll only know if this effort has succeeded when the curriculum and the tests are aligned to these standards."[95]

Other efforts in research and advocacy by Gates and his foundation - and their close allies at the US Department of Education - have aligned teacher evaluations with test scores as well. Thus the idea that these standards "have nothing to say about how teachers teach" is the biggest myth of all. The standards spell out what is to be taught, the curriculum tells you how to teach it, and the tests determine how well you did the job. The educational process has been "aligned" from start to finish, and if you are not with the program, you will soon be out of a job.

In the spring of 2014, Gates-funded "research" was being spun on the witness stand in the Vergara case to argue against teacher seniority protections.[96] In the absence of such protection, senior teachers, who also are more costly, are highly vulnerable.

Gates has also pushed the expansion of charter schools, ignoring the data that shows they have not, as a sector, shown significant advantages over public schools. And Gates has been a major proponent of mayoral control of schools, arguing that when just one person is in charge, change can be made more efficiently.[97]

But once again, the data has not been kind to this experiment, as careful research has revealed that the cities where these reforms were implemented fared worse than those not under the reform regime.[98]

In February of 2014, journalist David Sirota uncovered the fact that billionaire John Arnold had donated $3.5 million to PBS as a sponsor of a series promoting "pension reform."[99] Just as much of what is sold as "education reform" has proved to be a means of undermining and destroying public education, so "pension reform" is emerging as a means of de-funding employee pensions, in spite of the lack of a compelling economic argument to do so.

As a result of this exposure, PBS affiliate *WNET* has returned the billionaire's money.[100] But the show, influenced by these millions, will still air. I guess it is a win-win for the billionaire. The show was produced in line with his beliefs, and he gets to keep his money.

Bill Gates has exercised similar influence over myriad organizations in the field of education over the past ten years. The Gates agenda is clear, so if you are looking to fund a non-profit or "research" organization, you know what you need to say and do in order to qualify for funding. Support the inclusion of test scores in teacher evaluations, support the Common Core, and support charter schools. The millions continue to flow to organizations willing to further this agenda. One Gates-funded teacher leadership group even requires its members to sign a pledge in support of these policies.[101]

The thing that has been tricky about this assault on public education and teacher autonomy is that it has not been open or transparent. Nobody from the Gates Foundation would ever say "we want to destroy due process for teachers" or "we hope to undermine teacher autonomy." The language is all aimed in the other direction. The rhetoric is all about how wonderful and essential teachers are, and how they ought to be treated as professionals. Only when you see that they think paying and evaluating teachers based on test scores is the way to accomplish this, does the cognitive dissonance arise.

The National Board for Professional Teaching Standards (NBPTS) featured Bill Gates as the keynote speaker at their 2014 *Teaching and Learning Conference.*[102]

I went through the process to become National Board certified back in the year 2000, so I am familiar with the standards that the organization is built upon. The National Board has never defined teacher quality on the basis of test scores. Teachers are expected to show how they contributed to student growth by sharing portfolios and videos where their impact is evident. Standards make it clear that teachers are responsible for skillfully creating classroom community, for treating all students in an equitable manner, for responding to cultural differences, and for collaborating with others to help students learn. Most of these things are not captured by test scores, and are undermined when test scores become the over-riding influence on our work.

The National Board has received several grants from the Gates Foundation in recent years. In 2010, the organization actively participated in the Gates Foundation's *Measures of Effective Teaching* project, receiving $1,195,639 to score videos of teaching.[103] More recently, The National Board received a Gates Foundation grant in the amount of $3,743,337 "to support revision of the National Board certification process."[104]

Given the way in which Gates Foundation grants have influenced organizations that have received them, I wonder if the revised National Board certification process will include the use of student test scores or VAM metrics as part of teacher portfolios?

The best teacher leadership, just like journalism or any other endeavor that requires integrity, ought to be independent of the undue influence of corporate sponsors, even those willing to whisper praise in our ears. I hope the National Board guards this independence fiercely.

Chapter 9

Gates and Duncan Seek to Use Trust in Teachers to Promote Common Core

In March of 2014, National Board certified teachers (NBCTs) gathered in Washington for the National Board's annual *Teaching and Learning* conference. They were presented with a beguiling vision of teacher leadership from both Arne Duncan and Bill Gates. It is beguiling because it offers NBCTs an opportunity to grasp something that teachers desperately desire - a sense of authorship over their classrooms, and genuine influence over future education policy. But what is being offered calls into question the meaning of true leadership.

Here is what Duncan promised in his speech:

That's why Ron [National Board CEO Ron Thorpe] and I are working together on an initiative called Teach to Lead. Our aim is to encourage schools and districts, and hopefully even states, all over the country to provide more opportunities for genuine, authentic teacher leadership that don't require giving up a daily role in the classroom. And because this only works if superintendents and principals see it as part of the solution, they'll be involved from the start.

We will convene a group of teachers, principals, state Chiefs, teachers' groups and district leaders, among others. This group will take the steps necessary not to create white papers to decorate shelves -- but to foster real-world commitments on teacher leadership. This group will announce significant commitments from districts, teachers' groups, and others who want to be part of the solution to make teacher leadership real at scale -- using the ample existing body of work on this as a springboard for action. And I want you to hold us accountable at this event, a year from now, for what we've been able to accomplish.[105]

This initiative, unfortunately will not yield much beyond some plum positions, if I might employ my crystal ball. And if you think I am being cynical, well, I think recent history supports my pessimism.

It was just two years ago that Secretary Duncan launched a similar effort, called *Project RESPECT*.

Duncan stood before a teacher "town hall" in February of 2012 and said:

> So today, we formally renew this national conversation around the future of teaching. I am absolutely convinced that the future of the teaching profession and the future of our nation are inextricably linked.
>
> We look forward to hearing your ideas, following your leadership, and pursuing your vision.
>
> As we fight to strengthen our nation economically, as we fight for greater social justice through strong and genuine educational opportunity, the voice of teachers has never been more important.
>
> This new vision will not appear overnight. There will be areas of disagreement. It will proceed in different ways in each state and district. There will be no single formula for success.[106]

Who has been at the helm of education policy since 2009? How many times is Arne Duncan going to promise to give us that seat at the policy table? Over the past decade and a half we have seen the teaching profession steadily eroded. The Department of Education provides multi-million dollar grants to the already bloated *Teach for America*, while calling for higher standards for the teaching profession. Secretary Duncan says we should avoid teaching to the test, but *NCLB* waivers require that teacher and administrator evaluations give significant weight to test scores.

If leadership is appointed and anointed by those in power, then it can be revoked by those in power.

So if we want to be leaders, we are better off developing that status in a way that does not rely on such official designations.

Leadership suggests influence over others. That influence is not won easily. It does not come simply from the letters "NBCT" after one's name. It is earned from the work one does and the examples one sets, including judgment, integrity and independence. In a time when our institutions are often subject to unwise policies and pressures, that independence can come with a cost.

Bill Gates' speech at the conference gave a clear indication of the ends he envisions the leadership of NBCTs serving. He urged the attendees to take a leading role in defending the embattled Common Core standards:

> There are many voices in this debate but none are more important or trusted than yours.[107]

While Gates now sees that the public trusts teachers, he himself has never trusted teachers much at all, as evidenced by the scant involvement of teachers in drafting the Common Core standards in the first place.[108]

While he came to the National Board to ask their support for this project, and sent a handsome grant of $3.74 million in advance, [109] he has previously disregarded the work of the National Board, and the level of expertise within the teaching profession. In 2011, he and his wife wrote this:

> It may surprise you--it was certainly surprising to us--but the field of education doesn't know very much at all about effective teaching. We have all known terrific teachers. You watch them at work for 10 minutes and you can tell how thoroughly they've mastered the craft. But nobody has been able to identify what, precisely, makes them so outstanding.

> This ignorance has serious ramifications. We can't give teachers the right kind of support because there's no way to distinguish the right kind from the wrong kind. We can't evaluate teaching because we are not consistent in what we're looking for. We can't spread best practices

because we can't capture them in the first place.[110]

So to combat this ignorance, Gates came up with the Common Core standards and tests to measure student performance. And as he said in 2010:

Aligning teaching with the common core - and building common data standards - will help us define excellence, measure progress, test new methods, and compare results. Finally, we will apply the tools of science to school reform.[111]

Gates' March, 2014 speech to the National Board conference also made it clear where he thinks innovation will come from, and it is not from practicing teachers. A report on his speech in the *Washington Post* relays his message:

"Standardization is especially important to allow for innovation in the classroom," said Gates, who used an analogy of electrical outlets. "If you have 50 different plug types, appliances wouldn't be available and would be very expensive," he said. "But once an electric outlet becomes standardized, many companies can design appliances and competition ensues, creating variety and better prices for consumers," he said.

"If states use common academic standards, the quality of classroom materials and professional development will improve," Gates said. "Much of that material will be digital tools that are personalized to the student," he said. "To get this innovation out, common standards will be helpful."[112]

Our classrooms are now to be the sockets for the various devices that innovators are now working on. Teachers are there to put the plugs in the socket, and show the students how they work. But innovation is the domain of creators of mass-produced tools. Teachers and students are consumers.

A look at Gates-funded teacher "leadership" projects provides a clue about his vision for teacher leadership. *Educators 4 Excellence* requires prospective members to sign a pledge declaring their support for school choice, for the use of VAM in teacher evaluations, and elimination of seniority protection.[113]

When power and wealth are concentrated, the wealthy and powerful will always look for "leaders" willing to step forward to help them implement their visions.

However, when such leadership opportunities are controlled by those in charge, the people in these posts will never be allowed to challenge the privilege and prerogatives of the powerful. These "leaders" lack the capacity to speak independently, and thus have compromised their ability to speak truth to power.

The trust teachers are given is a precious thing, and it obligates us to exercise our consciences and independent judgment.

Teachers, students and parents need leaders who draw their strength from their integrity and actions. To take that trust, and use it as leverage to gain positions of privilege, appointed and rewarded by the powerful, is a betrayal of those who trust us.

Remember, if Bill Gates and the Department of Education trusted teachers, they would not have had the Common Core standards drafted by test makers instead of educators. If they trusted teachers they would not have created the pseudoscience of VAM to try to hunt down the "bad teachers" hiding amongst us. If they trusted teachers they would not create "teacher voice" organizations that require allegiance to their beliefs. If they trusted National Board certified teachers, they would not have disregarded their expertise until they needed it to sell their Common Core standards and testing system to the public.

Leaders lead. They do not allow themselves to be co-opted and bought off.

Part II

Dialogue With the Gates Foundation

I am now convinced that the simplest approach will prove to be the most effective -- the solution to poverty is to abolish it directly by a now widely discussed measure: the guaranteed income.... We are likely to find that the problems of housing and education, instead of preceding the elimination of poverty, will themselves be affected if poverty is first abolished.

Martin Luther King, Jr., 1967[114]

In March of 2012, I received an email from a highly placed individual in the Gates Foundation. This person asked for a private dialogue, and since I agreed to that request, I will not share any details of those initial exchanges. After several weeks of discussion, I suggested that perhaps a face-to-face meeting with members of the foundation's education team might be in order. That set the stage for a visit I made to Gates Foundation headquarters in July. Following that meeting, we agreed to exchange perspectives through a series of five blog posts.

What follows, with minor adjustments for clarity, are the five essays I offered in that dialogue. Links are provided to the Gates Foundation's five essays.

Chapter 10

How Do We Build the Teaching Profession?

In July of 2012, I traveled to Seattle and spent most of a day meeting with leaders of the Gates Foundation, discussing their work around education reform. I had been critical of the impact their agenda had had, but they expressed an interest in opening up a dialogue. This chapter was the first in a series of exchanges that were intended to explore some of the key issues in education. We planned a process where we would take turns posting our perspective on a given theme, followed by a response from the other party. The posts were carried both on my own blog at *Education Week*, and on the Gates Foundation's *Impatient Optimists* blog.[115] We asked everyone to join in what we hoped would be a lively discussion. The education reform debate has deteriorated at times—our goal was to engage in a constructive conversation, to turn down the heat, and to seek a bit more light. The first exchange focused on these two related questions:

How can educators create a strong professional culture in our schools?
How do we build the teaching profession?

The Gates Foundation has presented effective teaching as the focus of its education work for the past few years. Unfortunately much of the reform work during this time has focused on the negative side of the teacher-effectiveness equation. Reports like *The Widget Effect*[116] have built up the idea that American schools are places where nobody is ever fired. Films like *Waiting for Superman* have reinforced the concept that due process for teachers means we have "jobs for life." The Gates Foundation,

I believe, has actively promoted these ideas, and in 2010, Bill Gates stated on Oprah that if we could get rid of bad teachers, "our schools would shoot from the bottom of these (international) rankings to the top."[117]

But there seems to be a growing awareness that real growth will not come from this strategy of rooting out the bottom 5 percent of performers. For this first exchange, I wanted to explore what a healthy collaborative culture looks like, and how it relates to teacher evaluation.

Let's take a look at the best model of collaboration I have personally seen in recent years, the teachers at *New Highland Academy* in East Oakland.[118] This group of teachers worked with the support of a team at Mills College to engage in thoughtful inquiry into their practice. They met regularly to look at student work and talk about where their students were struggling. When they looked at their students' work, they saw that while the curriculum they were using was helping the students learn to decode, their comprehension was lagging. They chose a set of strategies to help their students to find meaning in what they read, and worked across the school to try this out.

Here is how teacher leader Aija Simmons explained it:

'The Answers' are what we all problematize. Because what 'the answer' is for me in this moment might not be the answer two years from now. So the good thing about inquiry is that I'm constantly understanding that there's a new question, this is a new group of students, it might work better than the last thing but I'm continuing to probe myself, so that I'm pushing myself to deeper understandings about how my students learn, and I'm coming back to the question. I have had several inquiry projects that I've looked at over the course of multiple years, but I use them as professional developments. People have the same question that you have, and as you come together, and you begin to think more and share your ideas of inquiry, and get more tools, we're moving ourselves forward.[119]

They saw tremendous results. But the biggest lesson was not just the results, but the ownership these teachers had of their own expertise. By engaging in this process, where THEY figured out the big challenges before them, and THEY figured out what to do about it and how to monitor their students' learning, they were acting as professionals.

The energy you see in these teachers is what happens when you give people autonomy and the time to use it. This energy is destroyed when mandates and models of professional growth are imposed from above.

This sort of research allows teachers to give one another feedback, and to reflect on their teaching practices. This feedback and reflection is most productive in a teacher-led collaborative context. It does not NEED to be a part of an evaluative process in order for teachers to learn and grow. Of course, evaluations should recognize and encourage this sort of work. But the most productive collaboration is peer-to-peer, of the sort done by the teachers at *New Highland Academy*.

When we look at our schools, we have to ask, what does it take to support this kind of innovation?

- **Confidence in teachers:** The principal at this school trusted these teachers to take on this challenge.

- **Active partners, and a model of inquiry:** These teachers were supported by the *Mills Teacher Scholars* program,[120] which helped them learn how to investigate their practice using the teacher inquiry process.[121] Another model that I have seen work well is *Lesson Study*.[122]

- **Autonomy and choice:** These teachers actively chose the form of inquiry they would pursue, and thoughtfully determined the line of inquiry they would follow.

- **Stability:** This project was led by experienced, expert teachers. This approach will not succeed in a school with high turnover.

- **Small class sizes:** Special funding has kept class sizes small at this high poverty school, which has made this work much more possible.

- **Time for collaboration:** Teachers cannot do this sort of work without dedicated time for collaboration.

This school has been supported by the *Quality Education Investment Act*,[123] a state funding program developed by the *California Teachers Association*. These funds allow for smaller class sizes, and that big essential, time for teachers to meet and reflect together.

This sort of process is destroyed by high-stakes tests and the micromanagement that comes with top-down mandates. It is crucial that teachers at any given site have the autonomy to choose the model of collaborative inquiry that fits both their culture and the challenges they face. Every time I have seen extraordinary leadership emerge from a staff, it has been when this autonomy was given. And every time I have seen top-down reforms come along, the energy drains away. We will not get this sort of professional culture without trusting and empowering our teachers to behave as true professionals.

Another model of professional growth was a mentoring program I started in Oakland, called *TeamScience*.[124] In existence from 2009 to 2013, this project paired veteran science teachers with novices, in order to both boost their effectiveness and retain them. This program was needed because of the district's reliance on programs like *Teach For America* to fill vacancies, especially in science, math and special education. Unfortunately, research has shown that 57 percent of the people entering TFA do not intend to make teaching their career, and in fact, three years after they start, three fourths of these teachers are gone from our schools.[125] Although we made a dent in the turnover rate, high numbers of these novices continued to rotate through our schools. Providing them with mentors has some short-term benefit, in terms of the quality of their instruction. But this investment is lost if these temporary teachers leave, taking their expertise with them.

Recent research on teacher turnover has revealed the high cost of instability:

> For each analysis, students taught by teachers in the same grade-level team in the same school did worse in years where turnover rates were higher, compared with years in which there was less teacher turnover.

> An increase in teacher turnover by one standard deviation corresponded with a decrease in math achievement of 2% of a

standard deviation; students in grade levels with 100 percent turnover were especially affected, with lower test scores by anywhere from 6 percent to 10 percent of a standard deviation based on the content area.

The negative effect of turnover on student achievement was larger in schools with more low-achieving and black students.[126]

To build the teaching profession we must recruit people who want to make a serious commitment to teaching, then support them with meaningful training. Why not subsidize people who choose to become teachers, and allow them to serve as half-time apprentices alongside excellent mentors? They could use the other half of their time to take courses in child development and pedagogy. Urban teacher residency programs offer models along these lines, but are not well supported.[127]

Unfortunately the Gates Foundation has been a big supporter of *Teach For America* in the past. If we are going to build the teaching profession and sustain solid collaboration at our toughest schools, we need to place a high priority on stability. Any program that encourages people to enter the classroom without a desire to stay beyond two years is a tremendous waste of time and energy.

What about teacher evaluation?

In an essay written in March, 2012, I tried to create a portrait of what a constructive evaluation process might look like:

A teacher meets with his or her evaluator. They review the professional standards in use, and look for areas in need of growth. Maybe it is a focus on literacy and writing skills. Maybe it is bringing the English learners level of engagement and participation up. They discuss strategies the teacher might try to address these things, and they also discuss the forms of evidence they will look at over the year to see what is happening in this area. Assessment, especially of the classroom-based formative sort, is a powerful tool. How is a teacher assessing his or her students' abilities? How are they using that information to give feedback and give the student appropriate, challenging work? This is where teachers use genuine assessment grounded in their understanding of their students. When this sort of assessment data is shared with an evaluator, a comprehensive portrait of how this teacher is helping students to grow can emerge.

Once an area of focus has been defined, the teacher and evaluator find some professional development resources that might help as well -- maybe a conference to attend, some books that might be read, a grade-level team that might come observe a lesson here and there and offer feedback, a colleague that is expert in this area to go observe. Then over the year, the teacher collects student work samples that provide evidence of learning. They document how they have designed instruction to help students learn, and show where they have provided feedback. The evaluator observes, a few times at random, and a few times by request, to see particular lessons. This evidence would be appropriate to the goal that has been set. It could include some test data, but test data would just be one source of evidence among many.[128]

In contrast, in Bill Gates' July, 2012 speech in Atlanta, he framed the problem this way:

Developing a great teacher improvement system is truly difficult—because there are no models. The country's teachers have been working in systems where almost everyone gets a good evaluation—and almost no one gets any feedback. That's the key point. Our teachers get no feedback—no guidance on how to get better.[129]

I disagree with this dismal appraisal. There is certainly room for improvement in teacher evaluation, but to say there are "no models" whatsoever is just wrong. Take a look at the report I worked on several years ago with fellow members of *Accomplished California Teachers*.[130] The model I described above is in action in the schools of Santa Clara, California.

Another model with which I have some experience is *Peer Assistance and Review* (PAR). I served for two years as a Consulting Teacher in Oakland's PAR program. I was tasked with observing and assisting teachers who had received poor evaluations. I was in their classrooms every week, and met often with them, offering feedback and resources to help them improve. I also took notes on what I observed, and in the spring

I wrote a report which was used as the basis of a recommendation from a joint union/administration committee as to the teacher's continued status. In most cases, the referred teachers were convinced to leave the system.

I discovered doing this work that, in most cases, my observations matched up with those of the evaluator. However, there were a few occasions where this was not true. Perhaps a personality clash or power struggle had led to an unfair evaluation. In several cases the teacher in question transferred and was successful under a new administrator. The PAR program provides some essential elements that are needed to create a trustworthy evaluation system:

- An initial check on the quality of the evaluations, which was often very uneven.

- Another pair of eyes, with expertise, observing a teacher's practice not just once or twice, but many times.

- A chance for improvement—specific feedback, resources and time to make changes.

Teachers who are referred to PAR can indeed be terminated if they do not succeed in the program, and the majority of those referred left the system one way or another, although many chose to take early retirement or resign rather than go through the termination process. The low number of actual terminations is at least part of the reason reports like *The Widget Effect* are so critical of PAR—but this is deceptive.

The PAR program gives crucial credibility to the entire evaluation process, as part of a system of due process. If you have chosen teaching as a career, you ought to have a real process before that career is ended by a few years of low VAM scores, or the un-verified opinion of one administrator.

The evaluation systems I described from Santa Clara and the PAR program are not new discoveries for the profession, though Gates is apparently unfamiliar with them. We educators need to elevate and share these effective practices, and create powerful themes for strong evaluations. We need to look at the places where these practices are in place, and share them. I believe we will find these models are undermined, not enhanced, by the use of VAM and other test-driven reforms.

Even as educators move to improve evaluations, we should discard the idea that useful feedback can only come in the context of a high-stakes evaluation. Just as our students learn best when we shift the focus of feedback away from grades, teachers learn best when feedback and reflection is developed in the context of peer-to-peer collaboration, not in the context of them being rated, ranked or categorized by an arbitrary VAM evaluation system.

So to summarize my views: We need to pursue the conditions necessary for solid reflective, collaborative cultures in schools. These are dynamic processes that rely on the leadership and inspiration of everyone involved. They require trust to be invested in our school leaders, who in turn need to trust their teachers to engage in this often open-ended work. Constant pressure to raise test scores and top-down mandates destroy this. These external pressures do not add coherence—they subtract it. Teachers need autonomy and time, and they need support, access to partners, the use of strong models of collaboration, and small class sizes so they are not overwhelmed every day. We need to strengthen, not eliminate due process, when we ask teachers to open their classroom practices to one another and reflect honestly about their practice.

The Gates Foundation's response to the points raised in this chapter was written by Irvin Scott. The written response, as well as their other posts in this exchange, are not included here but can be found online at *Living in Dialogue* and their blog, *Impatient Optimists*.[131]

Chapter 11

How Do We Consider Evidence of Learning in Teacher Evaluations?

The tricky question of how we look at evidence of learning was the next topic. The Gates Foundation's Vicki Phillips wrote the first essay,[132] and this chapter was my response.

Vicki Phillips opened her essay with a criticism:

Education debates are often characterized wrongly as two warring camps: blame teachers for everything that's not working in our schools or defend all teachers at all costs.

This handwringing is hard to take seriously, because, as I first wrote in 2010, there has indeed been a war on the teaching profession, and the Gates Foundation continues to arm one side very heavily.[133]

The Gates Foundation continues to fund *The Media Bullpen*, the *National Council for Teacher Quality*, *Teach Plus*, *The New Teacher Project*, and literally scores of other groups which not only carry on campaigns to undermine due process for teachers, but also actively lobby for coercive legislation that forces public schools to use faulty test scores for the purposes of teacher evaluation, against the best judgment of administrators and academic experts.

The Gates Foundation gave $2 million to promote *Waiting For Superman*, a movie rife with falsehoods about public education, which greatly promoted the hostile climate in which we find ourselves.

Ms. Phillips' essay focuses almost exclusively on the work of the *Measures of Effective Teaching Project*, an initiative of the Gates Foundation. While the Gates Foundation has invested heavily in this project,[134] this is just one small part of the work they fund in this arena. In 2013, *Education Week* estimated they have spent an estimated $700 million on their "teacher agenda."[135] We have not yet seen enough of the systems under development by the *MET* project to really understand them, so I will focus my attention on the other fruits borne by Gates Foundation investments.

The first question that arises when discussing teacher effectiveness is how we measure student learning. While Ms. Phillips distances herself from the use of test scores, this has been central to the reforms advanced by the Gates Foundation thus far. It is possible that the *MET* project will chart new ground, but before it does so, it will need to reverse all the policies and laws mandating evaluation systems that rely on test scores that have been passed at the insistence of the Gates Foundation and supported by the programs it has funded.

Researcher Walter Stroup has given the testing paradigm a much-needed shaking up in his 2012 report on the way standardized tests have been constructed, as reported in the New York Times.[136]

He focused on classes of students that had made significant strides in their understanding of math concepts. When he reviewed their standardized test scores, he discovered very little improvement, in spite of their learning gains. How could this be? He discovered that the test designer's goal was not to create a test that was sensitive to learning, but rather was to rank students, to reproduce the spread of outcomes that we expect. These tests are "insensitive" to a great deal of learning, and of little use in evaluating the quality of instruction. Therefore, when the Gates Foundation - and its myriad sponsored projects - insist that test data be our guiding star, we are often misled.

This is no surprise to teachers. The Gates/Scholastic survey of teachers found that only 28% of teachers see standardized tests as an essential or important gauge of student assessment, and only 26% say they are accurate as a reflection of student knowledge.[137] Another question reveals part of the reason this may be so - only 45% of teachers think their students take these tests seriously, or perform to the best of their ability.

Melinda Gates recently said on Nightline, "An effective teacher in front of a student, that student will make three times the gains in a school year that another student will make." Math teacher Gary Rubinstein did some digging to figure out[138] that the source of this statistic is a very weak twenty-year-old study by Eric Hanushek, an economist who has also "proven" that money does not matter in educational quality.[139]

The Gates Foundation has for years been paying for various studies and supporting think tanks that have aggressively promoted the use of merit pay as a means of promoting teacher effectiveness. Even as Florida teachers describe the new evaluation system there as "artificial" and "frustrating,"[140] Gates-funded outfits like the *Southern Regional Education Board* praise the state for their expanded data systems. The Gates-funded *National Council on Teacher Quality (NCTQ)* has begun issuing annual report cards on teacher preparation programs based in part on their enthusiasm for test data,[141] and the Gates-funded *Data Quality Council (DQC)* exerts similar pressure on states to expand their investments in testing and data systems.[142]

However, there seems to be a dawning awareness among a number of Gates Foundation scholars that some of the things the Gates Foundation says it wants, such as a trusting collegial environment where collaboration and constructive feedback are the norms, are undermined by a competitive, fear-filled environment where nobody is sure if they will have a job next year.

Here is the problem. Before we can begin to build the kind of positive collaborative culture we need in our schools, we have got to unwind the damage that the past decade has wrought on them.

We need to start with an understanding of what teachers can and cannot do, because this idea that good teachers can eliminate the achievement gap, and that bad teachers are to blame for much of it - is just wrong. In the first place, most research, even that of Dr. Hanushek, shows that the teacher is only responsible for about 10% of the variance in student performance. The lion's share goes to characteristics the students bring with them - their family's educational background, income level, neighborhood conditions, health care, and all sorts of issues that are closely related to poverty. This graph, from a 2013 study by Edward Haertel[143] gives an idea:

How Much Variance in Student Test Score Gains is Due to Variation Among Teachers?

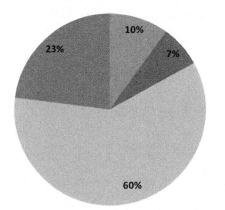

Influences on Student Test Scores

- Teacher: 10%
- Other School Factors: 7%
- Out-of-School Factors: 60%
- Unexplained Variation: 23%

So the starting point for our focus on "teacher effectiveness" is unwise, in a strategic sense. If the differences between teachers only account for less than a fifth of the differences we see in student outcomes, then putting all our attention there can't be seen as a useful effort. On the other hand, if the key difference in student outcomes is due to factors related to poverty and racial and economic isolation, then perhaps we would get better results by focusing there. In fact, the greatest gains made in closing the gap student achievement between African American and white students took place between 1970 and 1980, when anti-poverty and desegregation programs began to take hold. The past two decades have seen those programs disappear, and our schools have become re-segregated.[144] And the achievement gap has not budged, even as test-based accountability has made closing that gap its central goal.

But for the sake of this particular discussion, let's agree that teachers are important and can make a difference in the lives of our students. We want to be the best teachers possible in front of our students, and therefore we should do all we can to make this possible. As Walter Stroup pointed out, teachers have experienced a decade of high-stakes testing that is insensitive to a great deal of learning.

The work that has been done to enhance teacher effectiveness to date has been crippled by the willingness to use standardized test data as an adequate proxy for learning. In fact, we all want much more from our schools than can be measured on a test. Richard Rothstein, in his 2008 book "Grading Education, Getting Accountability Right,"[145] points out that we actually want the following things from our schools:

- Basic academic skills and knowledge

- Critical thinking and problem solving

- Appreciation of the arts and literature

- Preparation for skilled employment

- Social skills and work ethic

- Citizenship and community responsibility

- Physical health

- Emotional health

Of these, standardized tests only begin to measure the first. When high stakes are attached to these tests, all other goals become devalued. I saw this first-hand in the Oakland schools where the school board had to pass a directive telling elementary schools that they needed to teach science. Many of the low-income schools were spending two hours plus a day on reading, and another ninety minutes on math, leaving no time for science. The school board passed no such resolution about art or history, so these subjects continue to be left behind. This problem is intensified when we shift into a model where each and every teacher's scores are used as a significant part of their evaluation.

More recently, Bill Gates has been voicing a bit more caution about the wave of reforms his words and money have spawned. In a speech given in the summer of 2012, Gates publicly backed away from some other policies that his dollars continue to advance. On paying teachers for better test scores, all of a sudden he has no opinion:

> Now, let me just say that at this time, we don't have a point of view on the right approach to teacher compensation. We're leaving that for later. In my view, if you pay more for better performance before you have a proven system to measure and improve performance, that pay system won't be fair - and it will trigger a lot of mistrust. So before we get into that, we want to make sure teachers get the feedback they need to keep getting better.[146]

This is progress, I guess. Though I am not quite sure why, if Gates is aware of the potential harm many of the merit pay schemes are now causing, he does not oppose them, especially since many of them have Gates Foundation fingerprints on them. Furthermore, while he now professes no opinion about compensation systems, there is no apparent lack of confidence in Gates Foundation supported models for evaluation systems, which are even more dependent on an atmosphere of trust. And all these systems continue to go forward in legislatures across the country as a direct result of advocacy by various groups working under the Gates Foundation's sponsorship. All of these systems for teacher accountability - is there any accountability for the organizations responsible for these crazy evaluation systems?

There is a whole lot of research piling up that shows how ineffective paying AND evaluating teachers based on test scores has been.[147] There is no logical reason that the pressure we apply through compensation is any different from the pressure of a high stakes evaluation system. If we apply our understanding of pay to the issue of evaluation, perhaps we might get some insight. Daniel Pink says the best way to motivate people with money is to pay them enough to take it off their minds.[148] What if we looked at evaluations in a similar way? How do we make professional growth central? We need to remove the distraction created when high stakes decisions are triggered by unreliable VAM scores. And we need to make sure there are strong due process systems in place so that teachers are not in fear that their apparent "weaknesses" derived solely from VAM scores may be used to justify their unfair dismissal.

We know from the research of Paul Black and Dylan Wiliam described in *Inside the Black Box*[149] that students grow the most when they are focused not on the grades they might be earning, but rather on the quality of their work. How can teachers focus on the quality of their work if they are in a state of constant fear over losing their jobs if their students' test scores do not rise fast enough? This intense pressure, at the level of school and teacher, is very counterproductive when we want to promote the conditions for growth.

That does not mean nobody should ever be fired. But our schools, especially in high poverty areas, would be far better served by an emphasis on supporting and retaining teachers than it is being served by a campaign to weed out the supposed poor performers.

In the framework Bill Gates offered in his February, 2012, Op-Ed in the *New York Times*, he discussed the need for "multiple measures." Ms. Phillips echoes this in her post. Unfortunately, in a high stakes environment such as we now have, adding additional elements to a VAM evaluation system does not make the pressure to focus on test scores disappear. And I do not share Ms. Phillips' optimism that the new Common Core tests will somehow evolve beyond the limitations evident in every previous generation of standardized tests.

The model for teacher evaluation that the Department of Education has required for states to receive *NCLB* waivers lines up with the Gates Foundation's approach, and has required a "significant" portion of teacher AND principal evaluations to rest on student outcomes - which means test scores. This means in the states that have received those waivers, 30% to 50% of these evaluations rest on test scores. As Bill Gates said: "Test scores have to be part of the evaluation. If you don't ground evaluations in student achievement, evaluations will conclude that 'everyone is excellent,' and that holds teachers back."[150]

I will let the Gates Foundation folks explain the way they envision multiple measures working. They must understand, however, that their track record thus far does not inspire confidence.

Reformers have tied huge stakes to these evaluations. At the urging of those who have declared getting rid of "bad teachers" job one in our schools, many states have significantly weakened due process for teachers. As a result, faulty VAM based evaluations are resulting in career-ending decisions. The test score component is almost always going to be made up of VAM scores, which have been repeatedly demonstrated to be unreliable. The impact of these scores cannot be washed away by including student surveys and classroom observations to the evaluation process. And remember that often these observations will be done (or supervised) by principals, whose evaluations likewise now rest in large part on test score gains.

Let's take a close look at why VAMs are now being taken apart by education researchers and mathematicians.

As Linda Darling-Hammond's research has highlighted, students from low income, special education and English learners are consistently harder to raise on the VAM scales.[151] This creates serious disincentives that we are already seeing take effect in places that are using VAM - even though it may be only one of multiple measures. Teachers will seek to avoid these students. This is reality - not theory.

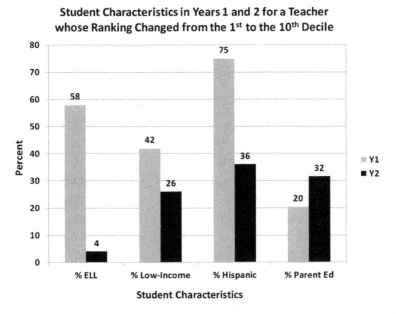

This figure was originally published by SCOPE in Creating a Comprehensive System for Evaluating and Supporting Effective Teaching, 2012. Printed with permission, Stanford Center for Opportunity Policy in Education.

This graph from Darling-Hammond's work illustrates the student characteristics of one teacher whose VAM scores showed a significant improvement from one year to the next. In the year when her students were almost 60% English learners, she was in the bottom tenth of teachers. The next year only 4% of her students were English learners, and she zoomed to the top tenth. This trend is repeated for low income and Hispanic students. Given these kinds of wide variations in VAM scores from one year to the next for the same teacher, who would choose to teach a class such as this teacher had in year one? And how long would any teacher last in a system where a VAM score was 40% or 50% of one's evaluation?

If you are not convinced of the problems with VAMs, please review this essay by mathematician John Ewing, who summarizes the many flaws once again in detail.[152] Two other reports worth reading are *Getting Teacher Evaluation Right: A Background Paper for Policymakers*,[153] and the statement from the American Statistical Association on using VAM for teacher evaluation.[154]

These VAM teacher evaluation systems are causing good teachers to be misidentified and hounded out of the profession.[155] And worst of all, these systems penalize teachers working with the most vulnerable populations of students, reinforcing their stigmatization, and making it even harder for them to get the teachers they need. This is not only unfair, it is terrible for students.

If the Gates Foundation wishes to reverse the effects of the war that has been so devastatingly waged against the teaching profession, it must first come to terms with the role it has played. Any attempt to dance around the very real damage that has been done invites dismissal by honest teachers. Evaluations that rely in any way on VAM scores are causing great harm to teachers and their students. If the Gates Foundation is unaware of this, after having spent millions studying how we can best measure effective teaching, I question its own capacity to learn. If the Gates Foundation IS aware of this, given its role in advancing these methods, it is not enough to simply come out with another, more nuanced model - while the old model continues to wreak havoc in our schools. If the Gates Foundation is accountable for its work, it must undo the harm to which it has, in major part, contributed.

The real "serious work" being done in education is not taking place in think tanks and research facilities. It's being done in classrooms in communities that are experiencing real and profound trauma. Yes, teacher evaluation ought to be all about reflection and growth. A great start would be to create the conditions that will make that growth possible, and to stop obsessing over test scores and measurement systems.

Chapter 12

Can Schools Defeat Poverty by Ignoring It?

It was my turn to post the first essay in this third topic, which involved the following two related questions:

What is the role of education reform in relation to the problem of family poverty? What is the best way to achieve greater equity in educational and life prospects for children of poverty?

The Gates Foundation's central slogan is "All lives have equal value," and the thrust of their work around education has been promoting institutional and political reform, based on the premise that this will increase equity, especially for the poor. The Gates Foundation has avoided systematic efforts to achieve equity of resources for schools and the children who attend them; instead, it asserts that teacher effectiveness is the best lever in this regard, and it has focused much of its research and advocacy on promoting public investment in systems that measure and promote teacher effectiveness.

In the name of reform, the Gates Foundation has wielded its political influence to effectively shift public funds, earmarked for the service of poor children, away from investment in those children's direct education experience. Through the *Race to the Top* and *NCLB* waiver conditions, the US Department of Education has instead dedicated public resources to creating state and federal mandates for the Gates Foundation's costly project -- making sure every aspect of our educational system is "driven by data." The future public expenditures required by the transition to the Common Core, with its greatly expanded assessment systems, will further deplete resources available for classrooms.

This is a huge error. In the US, the linchpin for education is not teacher effectiveness or data-driven management systems. It is the effects of poverty and racial isolation on our children.

As discussed in the previous chapter, the differences between teachers only account for less than 20% of the variance in student test scores, and more than 60% of test score variance correlates to out-of-school factors. We cannot solve the problem of educational inequity while we ignore the inequitable and inadequate resources available to low-income children in their homes and communities, as well as their schools.

In this chapter, I want to explore some of the reasons I believe we must take on the effects of poverty, based on my 24 years working in high poverty schools in Oakland, California.

First of all, let's take a closer look at what "out of school factors" really are all about. One of the central tenets advanced by many education reformers is that poverty is used as an excuse, a bogus justification for poor academic performance, which allows schools and teachers in poor neighborhoods to remain ineffective. Therefore, the best way to beat poverty in these circumstances is to set high expectations for everyone, hold teachers accountable for increasing test scores, and accept no excuses. So I want us to understand just what these schools, teachers, and children are up against.

First, the impact of violence:

This 2007 report in the *San Francisco Chronicle* described research done by the *Stanford Early Life Stress Research Program*:

As many as one-third of children living in our country's violent urban neighborhoods have PTSD, according to recent research and the country's top child trauma experts - early twice the rate reported for troops returning from war zones in Iraq....

PTSD can look a lot like attention-deficit disorder, ...with the lack of concentration, poor grades and inability to sit still. ...it almost guarantees that these students - often African American or Latino and low income - won't do as well on standardized tests as their wealthier, whiter and safer peers.[156]

Another researcher, Patrick Sharkey, reported dramatic drops in test scores for children who were exposed to violence:

> If a murder occurred in a child's neighborhood -- an area of roughly six to 10 square blocks as denoted by the U.S. Census -- the children's test scores fell by an average of half a standard deviation, Sharkey reported.[157]

In Oakland there were 131 homicides in 2012, and a map of their locations shows they occurred mainly in the African American and Latino neighborhoods where most of our students live and go to school.[158]

Second, health, housing and child development in poverty:

But violence is only one of the ways poverty intervenes in the lives of our students. Here are some others.

Early Vocabulary: The *Center on the Developing Child at Harvard University* reminds us:

> Early experiences and the environments in which children develop in their earliest years can have lasting impact on later success in school and life. Barriers to children's educational achievement start early, and continue to grow without intervention. Differences in the size of children's vocabulary first appear at 18 months of age, based on whether they were born into a family with high education and income or low education and income. By age 3, children with college-educated parents or primary caregivers had vocabularies 2 to 3 times larger than those whose parents had not completed high school. By the time these children reach school, they are already behind their peers unless they are engaged in a language-rich environment early in life.[159]

In Oakland, more than one in six children now lives in extreme poverty, according to the *2012 Kids Count Data Book*.[160] That means a family income of less than half the poverty level, which is set at $22,113 for a family of four.

Trina Shanks has done research that documents some of the affects poverty has on children.[161] Food insecurity hits children hard, especially infants, who may be developmentally delayed as a result of malnutrition. Stress from a variety of sources - parental unemployment, depression, inadequate housing, neighborhood violence, can rise to toxic levels that adversely affect children. This sort of stress can even have a negative effect on brain development.

In 2009, a short article in the San Francisco Chronicle carried this news:

> Almost 200 Oakland residents, including 74 children, were forced from their homes Tuesday after city officials condemned a refuse-strewn apartment complex in the 2500 block of Foothill Boulevard as unsafe, city officials said. The buildings had no running water, illegal wiring, boarded up windows and rodent infestations, officials said.[162]

Of course the 74 children living here were displaced - and shifted who knows where. But these children, up to that point, were presumably enrolled in their neighborhood schools, where they would arrive just like any other child. But unlike the children in wealthy neighborhoods, they did not go home to a safe house with warmth and running water.

The number of students receiving free or reduced price lunches has grown significantly, and in 2008-2009 44% of our nation's students were eligible. In the state of California, 52% are eligible. In Mississippi, 68% are eligible. In the city of Oakland, 68% of the students were eligible.[163]

It is estimated that 16 million children in America are at risk of hunger.[164]

One child in ten has been foreclosed upon. More than one million students are homeless.[165] More than two million Americans are incarcerated, and they are overwhelmingly the poor. One out of every nine African American children has a parent in prison. Incarceration has a significant negative effect not only on the person incarcerated, but also on their children.

As Michael Marder has illustrated so clearly, nothing makes sense in education without understanding the role of poverty.[166] This figure shows the way SAT scores in the state of Texas correlate with race and income.

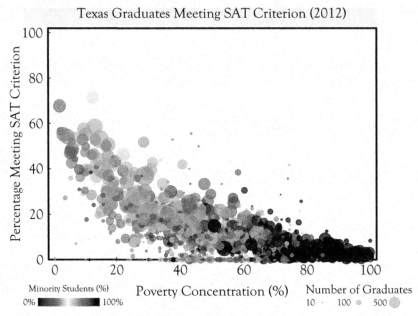

This figure was originally published by Michael Marder in "Education and Poverty" by Michael Marder on Prezi and is reprinted by agreement.

In global comparisons, the US leads in one area only, child poverty, with 22% of our children living below the poverty level.

This does not mean we should not seek the best teachers and schools for these children - of course we should. But it does explain why research shows that the difference between teachers only accounts for at most 15% of the variance in student test performance.

Third, what does this mean for teachers?

I have given a lot of statistics that demonstrate the impact of poverty on student outcomes at the broadest level. Let me describe what this looks like from the standpoint of a teacher in a high poverty school.

The school year starts and on day one there is a nice mix of students. They show up early, and sometimes parents even come by the classrooms poking their noses in to make sure everything is OK at the big middle school. Over the next few weeks another sort of student straggles in.

These are the ones who did not know school had begun, or did not think anything important would happen the first week. They do not have any materials, and when you tell them they need a pencil and binder every day, they say they do not have one. Attendance is spotty - sometimes there are little brothers or sisters to take care of, other times transportation issues, such as no money for the bus.

In one class I had about four students who were repeating the sixth grade. Some of them had also been held back in the first or second grade as well, so they were two years behind their peers. Many of these students have decided that they are not likely to win recognition as scholars, and are determined to get respect for their street smarts and toughness. Some of them have parents who are incarcerated, and thus live with other relatives, or in group or foster homes. I do my best to reach these students, to get them interested in doing experiments, to convince them that they have some talents that can be developed with practice. But it is tough going, and when the tests come around, most of these students show themselves to be significantly below grade level.

The description of behaviors triggered by violence rings true. Many of these students are diagnosed with Attention Deficit Disorder (ADD), and some are medicated so they can sit still in class. Often they are easily distracted, and this can create a steady stream of small disruptions in class, making it difficult for anyone to concentrate on the lesson at hand. Since they want respect for their toughness, sometimes they challenge my authority as the teacher to get it. The school's discipline and support systems are sometimes overwhelmed, and students that are sent out of class for disruptive behavior often return within a few minutes, with no change in behavior. There is pressure on the system not to suspend students, but there are few resources to respond to the underlying emotional needs of these children, so their trauma is managed, and their misbehavior is tolerated up to a point.

Fourth, this is a portrait of the reactions of the alienated and disenfranchised:

These are students who cannot believe in the American dream, because they do not see it reflected in their neighborhoods, homes, or the physical facilities at their schools. They see a different America.

Our education reformers want teachers to come into the schools like knights on white horses, plaster the walls with college logos, and push students to new heights with our high expectations. I have seen this attempted in dozens of classrooms of novice teachers, often associated with programs like *Teach For America*. We are pretending that there is some sort of level playing field here, but we are failing to create such a field. Instead, we just pretend these students are going to be able to compete with their well-heeled counterparts in the suburbs for shrinking higher educational opportunity. For most of them it is an empty promise.

At the end of the day, whatever advances teachers can make with their students are swamped by the statistical mix of unsupportable life circumstances, and progress is not "adequate." There will be a few individuals who emerge from this system as success stories, by luck, by extraordinary resilience, and through the dedication of their teachers. Education reformers elevate these exemplars to prove that "anyone" can make it, and condemn the teachers for failing to accomplish similar results for all their students. The whole system is built around the idea that anyone can make it and therefore we will ensure the highest level of success if we attempt to hold everyone to the same high standards, while largely ignoring the conditions in which they live.

Fifth, "impatient" reformers want schools alone to remedy the effects of poverty:

Back in the fall of 2010, I was part of an event at UC Berkeley called *Grading the Teachers*, where economist Eric Hanushek was a panelist. Dr. Hanushek said that if we could improve our scores to where Finland is, it would have a value to the US economy of $100 trillion. I interrupted to point out that Finland has a child poverty rate of about 2%. He responded:

> There is no doubt, no researcher that I know that has ever said, that family background [note that he refuses to use the term "poverty."] is not extremely important. It's not an issue. We understand that. We don't have the means to change families. Or we're not willing to use that as a nation. We DO have the means to adjust what our schools do. That's our public policy instrument. That's why some of us spend all of our time not looking at how to change families, but how to change the schools. There's absolutely NO evidence that if we gave

$10,000 a year more income to poor families that the achievement of those kids would increase. There's absolutely none. That's not to say we might not, for societal purposes, and I believe it, that we should worry about the income levels of the poor people. But not because that's the way to solve our school problems, or that we have to wait until we equalize incomes to address some of these achievement problems that are extraordinarily real.[167]

So this is the justification the "impatient" reformers use for disrupting and shutting down schools, dismissing whole staffs, and dislocating thousands of struggling poor children into other under-resourced buildings. We cannot WAIT to repair poverty. We have to tackle the problem where it is manageable and surmountable, in our schools. We cannot hold society accountable, so instead we will hold teachers and administrators accountable for their students' performance.

Academic performance has not improved under these mandated data-driven measures, and actual studies point to a decade of stagnation.[168]

Of course the country that Hanushek cited as our rival has taken an entirely different course of action. There, schools have not been left to handle these problems alone.

Former Director of Education in Finland, Pasi Sahlberg writes:

High-equity education in Finland is not a result of educational factors alone. Basic structures of the Finnish welfare state play a crucial role in providing children and their families with equitable opportunities for starting a successful educational path at age of 7. Early childhood care, voluntary free preschool (attended by 98%), comprehensive health services, and preventive measures to identify possible learning and development difficulties before children start schooling is accessible to all.[169]

The education system performance has to be seen in the context of other systems in society, for example, health, environment, rule of law, governance, economy, and technology. It is not only that the education system functions well in Finland, but that it is part of a well-functioning democratic welfare state. Attempts to explain the success of the education system in Finland should be put in the wider context and seen as part of the overall function of a democratic civil society.

Sixth, some reformers DO take on poverty:

The idea that we will create greater equity for the children now in our schools by raising standards, preparing them all for college, and holding their teachers accountable for their achievement is wrong and should be discarded. Children in poverty need much broader support for their development and learning that takes on the effects of poverty directly, of the sort suggested by the *Center for Mental Health* at UCLA.[170] The *Broader and Bolder Approach* offered a framework several years ago that suggests we address the effects of poverty and isolation as we pursue equitable outcomes.[171]

Advocates for equity have also launched the *Opportunity to Learn* campaign, highlighting many of these issues.[172]

We need greater prenatal programs to promote health of newborns. We need early childhood nutrition and education programs. We need to end the "war on drugs," dramatically reduce the levels of incarceration, and shift resources towards services for impoverished families. We need reforms that directly go after poverty, such as an increase of the minimum wage. The greatest reduction in poverty in our nation coincided with the expansion of collective bargaining for workers, so we should be supporting unionization, not just of teachers, but of all workers.

History shows that the greatest closure of the achievement gap took place during the years that the US took concrete steps to economically and racially desegregate schools. But in the past two decades this has been reversed, and now segregation is greater than it has been since the 1950s.[173] We hear the rhetoric of the Civil Rights Movement, but the reality is a reversal of many of the gains of that era, and a dramatically widening gap between the rich and the poor.

Perhaps not coincidentally, this is the same time that societal wealth has flowed ever more to the top one percent of our households. The heirs to the Walmart fortune have as much wealth as the bottom forty percent of American families.[174]

And the bank "bust" of the past several years has been paid for not by bankers, but by our cities, states and school districts.[175] This was a transfer of wealth from the ordinary public to the pockets of the already wealthy. With this loss of wealth, we are losing the power to democratically determine public education policies for our children. Our public schools are being systematically de-funded under "austerity" budgets made necessary by this theft of public resources.

While Bill Gates stated in 2012 that the wealthy should pay more taxes, it is hard to find evidence of this priority in looking at the grants the Gates Foundation has given. When Bill Gates spoke to governors the year before, he did not mention his desire to raise taxes on the wealthy. Nor did he mention the problems of poverty, nor did he encourage the governors to find the moral courage to defend funding for their schools, or services for the poor. Instead, he suggested that they might save money by increasing class sizes, and by ending the practice of rewarding teachers financially for obtaining advanced degrees.

Most of the projects supported by the tax-exempt Gates Foundation take a "money is not the answer" approach. Yet if our schools are to even begin to address inequities, we must begin by funding them adequately. Our nation's public school funding is in a shambles, and the schools attended by the poor are, by and large, funded at far lower levels than even the public schools attended by wealthier students. The *Savage Inequalities* that Jonathan Kozol wrote of two decades ago[176] are, shamefully, even worse.

The numbers tell the tale:

According to the National Center of Education Statistics, the wealthiest school districts spend far more per pupil than the national average. The Darien, Conn., public school district spends $15,433 per student per year, more than 50% above the U.S. average of $10,591. The Edgemont, N.Y., public school spends more than $25,000 per student annually. Barbourville, Ky., the poorest school district, spends less than one-third that amount.[177]

If money doesn't matter, why not spend our public assets on our neediest children, rather than those who come to school with the greatest advantage already? If class size does not matter, why do the schools of the privileged, including the school attended by the Gates family's children, have class sizes of around 16?[178]

The Gates Foundation's response to the points raised in this chapter was provided in a post titled *"Poverty Does Matter, but it is Not Destiny"*[179]

Chapter 13

What Is the Purpose of K-12 Education?

The fourth topic focused on the purpose for K12 education. The Gates Foundation's Irvin Scott went first, with a post titled "*K-12 Education: An Opportunity Catalyst.*"[180]

The exchange focused on these three inter-related questions:

What is the purpose of K-12 education? How do we think about college and career readiness? How do the Common Core Standards fit in?

In his essay, Irvin Scott of the Gates Foundation gave us some vivid images of the students he taught, and sincerely described the fervent desire that motivates every teacher - that we help those children entrusted to us reach their fullest potential. That is a drive that transcends this debate. And there we have common ground as educators.

However, when it comes to the broader strategy of the Gates Foundation, there remain some tough questions. The thrust of the Gates Foundation's approach is captured in this paragraph from Irvin Scott's post:

But we need all hands on deck when it comes to addressing poverty: we need there to be efforts laser focused on fixing the root causes of inequality that happen outside of school and we need efforts to focus on creating opportunity for all students in the classroom. By focusing on graduating college-ready students, we are empowering kids to have choices and opportunities that they otherwise would not have.

Thus far in our dialogue with the Gates Foundation, I had not seen much evidence of a "laser focus on fixing the root causes of inequality that happens outside of school." What I have seen is the laser focus on improving teacher quality through the use of evaluations that include test scores. And in this fourth post from the Gates Foundation we see their additional focus on college readiness as an antidote to social inequity.

I want to start by addressing the fundamental question we posed as our topic for this exchange. What is the purpose of K-12 education? Answering this question gives us some guidance in relationship to the shape of the reforms we pursue.

The purpose of K-12 education

Education fulfills our social obligation, as a people, to transfer the wealth of human knowledge to all our children. The goal of our public education system is to allow every child to develop his/her talent, and bring each one of them into full membership in our economic, cultural, and social community. This includes music, the arts, sports, physical and mental play, communication and expression. We prepare children to become active contributors to our culture and full participants in our democratic institutions.

We have PUBLIC schools to create a common space where children of all races, creeds and income levels gather to learn together. Our goal is not only to educate the individual, but also to build our ability to understand each other.

When I think of my own students in Oakland, my goal was not just to teach them the facts of science. I wanted to give them power in relationship to the world they encounter. I wanted them to be able to ask their own questions, and use the tools of science to investigate the world. Our disciplines of science, language arts, social studies, art and math are not just bodies of knowledge to be memorized. They are ways of interrogating and changing reality. History is an inquiry into the past that helps us understand our present and change our future. Language arts allow us to understand the writings of others, but also to express our own ideas in powerful ways.

Our students are growing up in a confusing world, where so many decisions have been made for them. The world is changing so fast, they need the most versatile set of tools possible. That means they need to be able to think for themselves, and do so with critical minds. The world MUST change because many of the ways we behave are not sustainable. Our students must be prepared not only to react and cope, but also to guide this transformation.

In the classroom this means teachers need the autonomy to figure out the best ways to get their students excited and engaged in their community, and in the world in which they live. They should be doing projects in which they tackle open-ended problems. They should be interacting with adults in their communities, with local businesses and academic institutions. The school should be a hub of community activity, and the students should be a source for solutions to community problems.

Robert D. Shepherd wrote in 2012:

1. People are extraordinarily variable, and

2. All have propensities to become very good at some things and not at others

In EVERY child some of these subsystems are extraordinary and some are merely adequate.

In other words, there are no standardized children. Almost every new parent is surprised, even shocked, to learn that kids come into the world extraordinarily unique. They bring a lot of highly particular potential to the ball game. And every one of those children is capable, highly capable, in some ways, and not in others.

Instead of schools having as their purpose turning out identically machined parts, what if they existed to find out what a given child is going to be good at doing? What if children were carefully, systematically, given opportunities to try out the enormous range of purposeful human activity until we identified each child's GENIUS? What if we said to ourselves, presented with a particular child, "I know that this young person is the product of 3.8 billion years of evolution, that he or she has gifts conferred by that history of fitness trials, and that it is my responsibility to discover what those are?"[181]

While education includes the knowledge and specific skill sets for economic participation, it should not be limited to the demands of current market conditions, or dictated by any calculation of the profitability of investing in our children. Each generation has the right to contribute to an economic system that serves its own human need. In our own age, whenever those who hold the advantage of wealth have used it to limit the boundaries of the lives of common people, societies have broken, or stagnated and crumbled.

Next, how do we think about college and career readiness?

Let's turn this question around: ***Is there a college or a career ready for them when our children finish their K-12 education?***

We have an obligation to assure that our economy meets the needs of the children we're educating. Skilled trades, service work, construction, retail, farming and agriculture, industry, transportation, high and low technology manufacturing, and health support are part of our economic reality. Children who are drawn to these livelihoods are entitled to educational preparation to share in the full responsibilities and benefits of our national life, including a decent standard of living for themselves and their families.

Irvin Scott makes it clear in his post that the primary strategy that the Gates Foundation has for combating poverty in the US is expanding the quality of teaching, and thus preparing larger numbers of disadvantaged students for college. Unfortunately, college readiness for all is no panacea. Getting people ready for college, and even significantly increasing the number who graduate from college, does not actually create the high paying jobs for these graduates. In order for these jobs to exist, we need some fundamental shifts in our economy. In order to raise the floor for those in poverty, we need to raise the minimum wage, stop outsourcing jobs, and increase the proportion of the workforce represented by unions. We need investments in the nation's infrastructure, and more equitable taxation, so the middle class has money to spend. Without changes like this, expanding the number of college graduates is likely to only lower their market value.

College for all?

Some people suggest that if we do not prepare all students for college, we will fall into the trap of tracking. Research shows tracking before age 15 is destructive, and associated with worse outcomes for the children and for society, both socially and academically.[182] The educational needs of children before that age aren't served by narrowing of the developmental and experiential mission of education to any track. By the later teens, actual career path options must be offered to children, which lead to real job futures for them, as well as access to higher education.

This doesn't mean that college has to be for everybody, but it requires that college be for **anybody**, and that the path to college and beyond be open to all.

Unfortunately, in the world where many of our students live, the path to college is closing off. Student debt has now surpassed credit card debt, and more than a trillion dollars is now owed.[183] Incredibly, this debt was only $100 billion as recently as 2010.

The cost of attending a state university has increased by 72% between 2001 and 2011, faster than even medical costs have risen. According to a 2012 article in the New York Times, "If the trends continue through 2016, the average cost of a public college will have more than doubled in just 15 years."[184] Two thirds of graduates take out loans, and the average debt is $23,300. Homelessness and hunger is a rising problem on college campuses.[185]

Rhetoric about "college for all" is hollow when society disinvests in higher education, and turns student loans into a profit center for the banking industry.

Furthermore, wages for college graduates are not inextricably linked to the level of education - they are a function of the marketplace. This report from 2012 showed that corporate profits were climbing at steep rates, while both wages and the number of people employed continued to decline.

So, how do the Common Core standards fit in?

The Gates Foundation has been driving a grand vision of systemic change, on the largest scale possible. Every reform is judged by whether or not it can be replicated and scaled up. This has led them to embrace standardization, enforced by high stakes tests, as the ultimate reform.

In my 24 years in Oakland, I saw several waves of top-down reform sweep through, usually guided by a similar idea. The idea is seductive. Here is how it works. First of all, we declare everything that is now being done a failure, because obviously we do not have the results we want. Anyone who wants to defend their work is "defending the status quo," which is unacceptable. The new strategy is brought in with great acclaim, and we are told that extensive research has proven that it works, but only if implemented "with fidelity." All the instructional leaders in the District are trained and sent out to proselytize, and principals are made responsible for implementation. Everything must be aligned to the new system.

Nationally, we have endured a decade of the most misguided, intrusive education reform ever. Thus it is not surprising that many teachers are in favor of what has been sold as the antidote. I am glad to hear the positive news from Hillsborough, and I hope teachers there feel empowered as they participate in the processes Mr. Scott describes. But oftentimes teachers are experiencing a different flavor of management - and we must be aware of that as well.

Here is a story from a teacher named Adam Heenan in Chicago:

Over the summer, teachers were asked to develop performance assessments aligned to the Common Core Standards. In some cases teachers were paid for their extra work, but in many cases, educators volunteered their time because they really wanted home-grown performance- and portfolio-based assessments. Those with whom I have talked - more than twenty- were excited that they were finally being deferred to on assessment development, that they felt that they were being treated as professionals, and they were glad to participate. They worked long hours over the summer, were proud of what they had created, and were excited to use it this year.

On Aug. 6th, teachers went back to school for five days of professional development. Over the course of that week, curriculum and instruction changes were implemented unilaterally, from the top-down. A very clear example is in a school on the southwest side where AP courses were taken away and replaced with remedial reading courses. The instructors were given 12 boxes of books with canned curricula from Pearson Education. It seems as CPS made a contract with Pearson behind the teachers' backs. Immediately all the teachers who had worked so hard over the summer to develop great assessments and aligned units, saw how CCSS was a 'Trojan horse,' for standardized curricula.[186]

The promoters of the Common Core will assert that the standards only offer the framework, and that teachers are still responsible for designing lessons and delivering instruction. But as our colleagues in Chicago discovered, in the top-down world driven by high stakes assessments, standards become mandates, and these mandates are best served by packaged curriculum. Teacher autonomy becomes a quaint relic. That is the experience of many teachers in high poverty districts and schools.

I want to draw attention to the work of an excellent thinker regarding education reform. Doug Christensen was the Commissioner of Education in Nebraska, a state that resisted the grips of *NCLB* longer than any other. They did this through a system of assessments that were developed at the district or regional level. In Dr. Christensen's view:

> Assessment and accountability must have their locus of action and policy at the local level and in the hands of educators and local policy leaders. Name a profession that is not in charge of their own metrics of success and the metrics of what is good practice? Lawyers are in charge of theirs. Medical doctors are in charge of theirs. So are accountants, nurses, bankers, and even morticians. Why aren't educators? Why aren't the local folks in charge and accountable?[187]

The other problem the Common Core is supposed to fix is the well-documented narrowing of the curriculum that has occurred as a result of *NCLB*. The answer in this case is to greatly expand the subjects that will be tested. There will be new tests rolled out over the next few years covering almost every subject, almost every grade level.

We will also see a greater emphasis on the "college readiness" component. This drive is already being used to justify tests for students starting as early as kindergarten. The Gates Foundation has funded *ACT, Inc*, which is partnering with Pearson to offer the "next generation" assessment system, which will indicate if "students are on track for success in college and 21st century careers."[188] These tests "will be delivered using state-of-the-art, digital platforms." They will be closely aligned with the Common Core standards.

How will this affect our students? Already we are seeing the impact of this sort of pressure on schools. A report from the *Alliance for Children* found this:

> When Walter Gilliam, head of the *Child Study Center* at Yale, surveyed almost 4,000 teachers from state-financed preschools, he learned that three- and four-year-old children were being expelled at three times the national rate for K-12 students. And 4.5 times more boys were being expelled from preschool than girls.

> Research is showing the critical importance of play for young children. In the 1970s Germany embarked on a similar plan to push early learning--turning its kindergartens into centers for cognitive achievement. But a study compared 50 play-based classes with 50 early- learning centers and found that "by age ten the children who had played excelled over the others in a host of ways. They were more advanced in reading and mathematics and they were better adjusted socially and emotionally in school. They excelled in creativity and intelligence, oral expression, and 'industry.' As a result of this study German kindergartens returned to being play-based again."[189]

The same report also found that we are losing creativity as a result of this drive:

While schools focus on drilling literacy and math skills into young children, a few researchers are studying what is being lost. Creativity is one casualty. The Torrance creativity test, which has been given millions of times over five decades in over 50 languages, is a better predictor than IQ of which students will become successful innovators in a host of professions. When Kyung Hee Kim at the College of William & Mary analyzed almost 300,000 Torrance scores of children and adults, Newsweek reported in 2010, "she found creativity scores had been steadily rising, just like IQ scores, until 1990. Since then, creativity scores have consistently inched downward. 'It's very clear, and the decrease is very significant,' Kim says. It is the scores of younger children in America--from kindergarten through sixth grade--for whom the decline is 'most serious.'"

This decline in creativity corresponds with warnings from Yong Zhao, who has pointed out how the US is in danger of killing the creative goose that laid our economy's golden eggs. At the same time we are embracing testable standards as the route to success, educators in China are doing their best to escape the trap of high stakes tests. And as Yong Zhao points out, high scores on the international PISA test have not yielded economic growth, but actually correlate with diminished innovation and entrepreneurship.[190]

In 2010, when Secretary Duncan described the many ways the Common Core would improve things, he made it clear that we would fix the problems created by *NCLB*'s high stakes tests by creating even more tests:

> For the first time, teachers will consistently have timely, high-quality formative assessments that are instructionally useful and document student growth--rather than just relying on after-the-fact, year-end tests used for accountability purposes.

> For the first time, state assessments will make widespread use of smart technology. They will provide students with realistic, complex performance tasks, immediate feedback, computer adaptive testing, and incorporate accommodations for a range of students.

Furthermore, Duncan said:

> Our proposal to reauthorize the Elementary and Secondary Education Act also would allow states to include subjects other than math and English language arts in their accountability system because we specifically want to foster the teaching of a well-rounded curriculum.[191]

So we will have more frequent tests, and more technologically sophisticated tests, requiring huge investments in testing software and computer hardware, and we will test more subjects, so that these subjects will also become driven towards test preparation.

As John Merrow wrote in 2012:

Companies like Pearson are getting rich while we blather and battle. They step into the vacuum and measure everything that's measurable. We should be measuring what counts, instead of counting whatever we are able to measure.[192]

Just to remove any doubt, I do not share the Gates Foundation's apparent faith in the ability of new technology to solve the problems the previous generation of testing technology created. The problem is not in the shape of the bubbles or the Scantron forms. The problem is that we are trying to improve teaching in the backwards way that a data driven system requires. Instead of challenging our teachers each day to find the best ways to engage their students, we are giving them lists of standards and scripted curricula to meet those standards. We replace the expectation that teachers will excite and inspire their students to take on new challenges, with the expectation that they will deliver a predetermined lesson, where even the student responses are anticipated and planned for. This is not the elevation of the teaching profession - it is its intellectual demise.

We have had more than a decade of test-driven accountability, and we have very little to show for it. Our schools should not be re-purposed into places for test preparation, even if those tests are now to be taken on computers. If the internet has taught us anything, it is that putting words and numbers through a microprocessor does not render them somehow smarter.

We need to re-examine our goals, and realize that our schools are not ecosystems walled off from the economy and society. They are porous places, and we must have strong connections with the needs and challenges in our communities. Our communities should play a strong role in supporting our schools, and making sure that the curriculum there is preparing students well for life beyond high school. Our schools should be accountable to parents, students and their community, not to a national testing system, no matter how technologically advanced.

In his post for the Gates Foundation, Mr. Scott writes:

> We believe that despite a child's circumstances, she should be given every opportunity to succeed and lead a life better than the one she was given. That is in direct contrast to the belief that because of a child's circumstances she is destined to live a life of obstacles regardless of the opportunities she's given. In our opinion, the purpose of K-12 education is to help provide and shape those opportunities.

Here is my problem with this statement. Mr. Scott states that the first sentence is a "direct contrast" to the second, when it is not. In fact, *both* sentences are true. We want to give every child every opportunity to succeed. *and* children who are raised in poverty live a life strewn with obstacles to their success. The first idea does not do *anything* to invalidate the second. Obstacles can and will be surmounted by a lucky or resilient few, but those obstacles will foreclose opportunities for far too many. Therefore providing educational opportunities is wonderful, but if we ignore the obstacles our students face, even as those obstacles mount, we are not truly taking on the challenges we face in our communities.

Returning to our students, I think we find common ground in the idea that as educators we want to equip them with the best preparation possible for their future, we want as many as possible to have a real opportunity to attend college, and we want them to live happy, productive lives -- whether they attend college or not. I have a deep concern about the de-funding of the public universities that is pricing college beyond the reach of many of our students. Whether students are headed for college or not, the Common Core standards will not serve them well if they are tied to high stakes tests and an overly prescriptive curriculum. Our teachers need the room to be creative if we expect them to inspire innovative thinking from their students. And I believe that our economy must be re-shaped if we are to have real opportunities for the next generations. As admirable a goal as it is, simply graduating them ready for college is not enough. I hope this dialogue leads us to look for deeper solutions.

Chapter 14

What Happens When Profits Drive Reform?

This was the fifth and last exchange in my formal dialogue with the Gates Foundation. The tension uncovered by this dialogue reveals a disconnect between the work of the Gates Foundation and many of us who have spent our lives working in schools. Nonetheless, this represents an opportunity to move beyond the impasse. Similar to the polarization that has occurred in the national political scene, the battle lines over education reform have become so hardened that it seems as if we cannot even agree on a common understanding of reality. Therefore bridging our differences requires us to share and discuss those realities, even though our perspectives are very different. I hope that this dialogue will deepen, and that the tensions that have been revealed will not lead us throw up our hands and abandon the effort, but rather will strengthen our commitment to continue to wrestle with these issues in the interest of our students.

In this final exchange, we tackled a big question:

What is the role of the marketplace in pushing forward education improvement and innovation?

In the fall of 2012, at the Republican National Convention, Jeb Bush used this analogy to talk about schools:

Go down any supermarket aisle - you'll find an incredible selection of milk.

You can get whole milk, 2% milk, low-fat milk or skim milk. Organic milk, and milk with extra Vitamin D. There's flavored milk-- chocolate, strawberry or vanilla - and it doesn't even taste like milk. They even make milk for people who can't drink milk.

Shouldn't parents have that kind of choice in schools?[193]

Choice has emerged as the solution at the same time that the public schools have been actively portrayed as an abject failure. How did we get here?

First, place public education in the crosshairs

Over the past decade, *No Child Left Behind* has left schools, especially those serving children living in poverty, battered and scarred. Why would people who supposedly want to improve schools treat them this way? There is a deep belief held by many conservative business leaders that schools will only improve when the "government monopoly" is broken and market forces are brought to bear.

As *Time* magazine reported in 2008:

...many early critics insisted that No Child Left Behind was nothing more than a cynical plan to destroy American faith in public education and open the way to vouchers and school choice.

Now a former official in Bush's Education department is giving at least some support to that notion. Susan Neuman, a professor of education at the University of Michigan who served as Assistant Secretary for Elementary and Secondary Education during George W. Bush's first term, was and still is a fervent believer in the goals of *NCLB*. And she says the President and then Secretary of Education Rod Paige were too. But there were others in the department, according to Neuman, who saw *NCLB* as a Trojan horse for the choice agenda -- a way to expose the failure of public education and "blow it up a bit," she says. "There were a number of people pushing hard for market forces and privatization."[194]

This campaign is now well under way, fueled not only by the ravages of *NCLB*, but by its more recent incarnation, *Race to the Top*, which required that states lift caps on charter schools to qualify for special

Federal funding.

Among those who have been working towards this were the leaders of the Thomas B. Fordham Foundation. Their five year report from 2001 explains the approach, which embraced:

> ...today's most promising education reform strategies: "standards-based" reform (with its trinity of academic standards, tests, and consequences for success and failure) and "market-style" reform (with its emphasis on school choice, competition, alternative providers, and accountability to clients). Some think these strategies are opposed or incompatible. By our lights, just the opposite is true: Each needs the other if it is to have the brightest prospect of succeeding.

> We shun two other popular theories of education reform that, in our experience, simply do not work to change institutions, alter behavior, or boost academic achievement. More money--absent standards and markets—won't make a difference. It's just paying the same people more to do the same things. And we've seen little evidence that the addition of more "expertise" to the present system will by itself bring about the needed reforms. That's because, with rare (and happy) exceptions, the present system does not much want to change. Hence we favor strategies that, in effect, force it to.[195]

Here is how this approach works. Impossible-to-meet, ever-rising test targets have been used to "prove" that the public schools are failing. This message is reinforced at every opportunity, and the schools are even wrongly blamed for problems in the US economy.[196] The supposed "failure" of the public schools then creates the "market" for alternatives, and legislators shift funds away from public schools towards all sorts of charter schools, virtual schools and even parochial schools.

This has unfolded largely according to plan. We saw the storyline played out in the 2010 pseudo-documentary "*Waiting For Superman.*" The public schools, burdened by unionized teachers impossible to fire, are failures, and the only salvation for students is in the scrappy charter schools that make no excuses.

One under-reported aspect of the Common Core national standards is that once they are implemented, the results will further accentuate disparities in achievement between states. Indeed, investors are already eying the opportunities this will create in the states revealed to be "behind" in their performance on Common Core assessments.[197] One slide in this investment advisor's 2102 presentation proclaims excitedly: "Help Close the Performance Gap! If Common Core has teeth, the 'Performance Gap' will get a lot bigger!"[198]

Second, make data profitable

In the Gates Foundation's vision for a well-engineered education system, data is the driver. Therefore profit-making partners are needed to manage the data that is needed to measure performance of everyone in the system. The Gates Foundation has even emerged as a sort of market broker to encourage this. This led the Gates Foundation to partner with a new non-profit organization, the *Shared Learning Collaborative LLC*, as Vicki Phillips explained in 2011:

> As part of our contribution, the foundation took an important first step a few weeks ago and selected a vendor to build the open software that will allow states to access a shared, performance-driven marketplace of free and premium tools and content. That vendor, *Wireless Generation*, will create the software, but it will be owned by an independent nonprofit, so that any school, school district, curriculum developer, or tool builder can contribute to the collaborative.[199]

A "free and premium tools and content system" typically means that bare bones tools will be offered for free, but districts will need to pay for full service versions. The *Shared Learning Collaborative* became *inBloom*, which declared itself out of business in the spring of 2014, as a result of opposition from parents concerned about student privacy.

The Gates Foundation has also formed a partnership with the Pearson Foundation to develop "cutting-edge learning resources" aligned with the Common Core standards.[200]

Third, invest in charter schools

In his 2009 Annual Letter, Bill Gates explained:

Based on what the foundation has learned so far, we have refined our strategy. We will continue to invest in replicating the school models that worked the best. Almost all of these schools are charter schools. Many states have limits on charter schools, including giving them less funding than other schools. Educational innovation and overall improvement will go a lot faster if the charter school limits and funding rules are changed.[201]

The Department of Education agreed with this thinking and required that states remove caps on charter schools as a condition for receiving *Race to the Top* funds.

When school districts sign something referred to as the "*Gates Compact*", they can get a special grant of $100,000, and be eligible for millions more, if they agree to open their doors to charter schools, and treat them the same as public schools.[202]

Unfortunately, a 2009 study which compared charter schools to nearby public schools, found them no better, and in many cases a bit worse, than the regular public schools.[203]

But more disturbing have been a number of recent reports focused on the ways in which the market has incentivized shortcuts to success, and even corruption.

The *Capital Roundtable For-Profit Education Private Equity Conference*, held in July, 2012, shared this on the conference web page:

Education is now the second largest market in the U.S., valued at $1.3 trillion. So while an industry of this size will always be scrutinized by regulators, the most onerous recent changes are likely over, and investors should face an easier climate down the road. And while eventual passage is not guaranteed, several pieces of legislation favoring the for-profit industry have been proposed in Congress.

In the K-12 space, the federal *Race To The Top* initiative has enabled a growing level of privatization in the K-12 segment, and rewarding districts for embracing alternative models, technological advances, and locally-based criteria.

Schools in these states have more flexibility in how they spend federal funds to benefit students, which benefits for-profit companies focusing on high-quality programs and services.[204]

The opportunity to make money has attracted lots of entrepreneurs towards education as a profit center. The testing companies were in on the ground floor, and have been active in supporting test-based reforms for years. The *Pearson Education Foundation* was fined for flying legislators around the world to education conferences, in advance of decisions they made granting Pearson lucrative test contracts.[205] In the years since then-governor Jeb Bush created the *McKay Scholarship Fund*, hundreds of millions of tax dollars have flowed to schools with little to no oversight, leading to widespread fraud.[206]

In 2012, the Associated Press reported that charter schools are leaving special needs students behind. The article says:

> Most charter, parochial and magnet schools serve children with disabilities, but they are often milder disabilities, leaving the brunt of students with significant needs in traditional district schools.[207]

Charter schools have also been faulted for various forms of selection. Most draw from a pool of parents who are seeking them out. Some have requirements for parental support and participation, which excludes some students. And some, such as the KIPP schools, have been found to have higher than average rates of attrition, meaning students who are **not** making the grade are transferring back into the public schools, something I witnessed in Oakland.[208]

Charter schools have also been having the effect of expanding the level of racial segregation. The 2010 report by the Civil Rights Project of UCLA reported:

> While segregation for blacks among all public schools has been increasing for nearly two decades, black students in charter schools are far more likely than their traditional public school counterparts to be educated in intensely segregated settings. At the national level, 70 percent of black charter school students attend intensely segregated minority charter schools (which enroll 90-100 percent of students from under-represented minority backgrounds), or twice as many as the share of intensely segregated black students in traditional public schools.[209]

One problem with turning education into a hotbed of entrepreneurship is that many advocates of "reform" also stand to make big profits. In this environment, it is hard to tell if the objective is better outcomes for students, or simply more dollars on the bottom line. One arena that appears highly profitable is online education - often offered through "virtual charter schools." Legislation that would require states to allow or even require students to take online courses has been promoted recently by the *American Legislative Exchange Council (ALEC)*. Jeb Bush has vigorously promoted this, according to this 2011 report by *The Investigative Fund*:

> The nonprofit behind this digital push, Bush's Foundation for Excellence in Education, is funded by online learning companies: K12 Inc., Pearson (which recently bought Connections Education), Apex Learning (a for-profit online education company launched by Microsoft co-founder Paul Allen), Microsoft and McGraw-Hill Education among others.[210]

In September of 2012, the *Portland Press Herald* published an expose entitled "The profit motive behind virtual schools in Maine." This report states:

> ...a partnership (was) formed between Maine's top education official and a foundation entangled with the very companies that stand to make millions of dollars from the policies it advocates.

> In the months that followed, according to more than 1,000 pages of emails obtained by a public records request, the commissioner would rely on the foundation to provide him with key portions of his education agenda. These included draft laws, the content of the administration's digital education strategy and the text of Gov. Paul LePage's Feb. 1 executive order on digital education.

> K12 Inc. donated $19,000 to [Maine Governor] LePage's election campaign through a political action committee. K12 and Connections Education provided support to Jeb Bush's foundation and to a controversial corporate-funded organization for state legislators, the American Legislative Exchange Council, or ALEC. Both K12 and Connections Education built relationships with Maine lawmakers and

officials who introduced laws and policies beneficial to the companies' bottom lines.[211]

And as Gary Miron has reported, the nation's largest "virtual school" chain, *K12 Inc*, has very weak academic results, in spite of outstanding revenues and a CEO with a $5 million salary.[212]

The role of the Gates Foundation

So how does all this inform this dialogue with the Gates Foundation? From my perspective, the drive for profits is problematic as a motive force for school reform. As we see with the virtual charter school sector, there are great incentives to create "efficiencies," and, lacking significant oversight, there are huge problems with quality. The collusion between the profiteering virtual charters, the testing industry, *ALEC,* and the legislative bodies that are being influenced through legalized bribery, taints the entire project.

The Gates Foundation has had a seminal role in many of the groups that have advanced both parts of the education reform formula - the high stakes testing that has been used to discredit public schools, and the market-based solutions we have been sold as the alternative. The Gates Foundation has funded most of the market-based reform groups described below:

- The Gates Foundation gave $2 million to publicize *Waiting For Superman.*

- Jeb Bush's *Excellence in Education* has been funded by the Gates Foundation for a number of years,[213] and in 2012 received a grant for $151, 068 "to complete a statewide communications campaign in Florida delivering the message on why there is a drop in school grades, why it is temporary, and how raising the bar on education standards leads to greater student success."[214]

- You have probably heard of the "parent trigger" movie, *Won't Back Down*? The organization that initiated the idea, *Parent Revolution,* started in 2009 with funding from the Gates Foundation.[215]

- The Gates Foundation has funded the *Media Bullpen*, which issues "grades" to the media based on how supportive they are of market-based reforms such as vouchers and charters.[216]

- The Gates Foundation also funded the creation of the *Cities for Education Entrepreneurship Trust*, which launched stating: "CEE-Trust's goal is to accelerate the growth of high-impact entrepreneurial education solutions in member cities across the country."[217]

- And although the Gates Foundation announced they would not extend future funding to ALEC, their grant of $376,635 remained in effect:

  > ...to educate and engage its membership on more efficient state budget approaches to drive greater student outcomes, as well as educate them on beneficial ways to recruit, retain, evaluate and compensate effective teaching based upon merit and achievement.[218]

The Gates Foundation funds a tremendous amount of activity in the education sector, and I am not suggesting that every project, or every person who takes funding from the Gates Foundation, is a partisan in this campaign. The Gates Foundation has funded many organizations that have done good work - but to be clear, there is no real "balance" here. Even though the Gates Foundation occasionally gives grants to the teacher unions, it is to fund projects aligned with the Common Core standards, or efforts to support "collaboration" with administrators. It is never - as far as I know - to fund efforts to de-emphasize standardized tests, or defend due process for teachers.

Finally, public schools are a public trust

Our public schools are one of the cornerstones of democratic life in our country. They exist not only to provide opportunity for individual students, but also as a common resource, in which we invest as community members. We bring together children from all races, religions and walks of life under one roof, to learn together.

We have seen what has happened to our health care system when it is driven by profit. People who are high risk cannot get insurance, and die without treatment. The same thing is happening to children walled off from educational excellence, shunted into dead end schools. For all the proclamations about education being the civil rights issue of our time, the marketplace does not fix inequity - it makes it worse. The children of the poor are more likely to have special needs and be more expensive to educate, and thus less likely to be served by profit-seeking charters.

Choice in education is an illusion. In some cases it allows a lucky few access to a better school. But the people and businesses seeking profit rarely want a level playing field - they seek whatever advantages they can get, and often that means leaving behind the special education student and the English learner.

As a parent, I was not only concerned about my own sons. I wanted the best education possible for all the children of our community. The public schools were a legacy handed to us by the generations before that built them. It is our challenge to rebuild them into places that fulfill that now tarnished ideal, and to educate everyone well. It is critically important that institutions such as our schools be driven not by decisions based on what is most profitable, but instead by our interest in the common good, and by our commitment to providing excellent opportunities for every child, even when this is unprofitable.

In the process by which decisions are being made about our schools, private companies with a vested interest in advancing profitable solutions have become ever more influential. The Gates Foundation has tied the future of American education to the capacity of the marketplace to raise all boats, but the poor are being left in leaky dinghies.

Neither the scourge of high stakes tests nor the false choices offered by charter schools, real or virtual, will serve to improve our schools. Solutions are to be found in rebuilding our local schools, and in recommitting to the social compact that says: in this community we care for all our children, and we do not leave their fate to chance, or to a lottery for scarce slots. We have the wealth in this nation to give every child a high quality education, if that is what we decide to do. With the money we spent on the Bush tax cuts for millionaires in one month, we could hire 72,000 more teachers for a year. It is all about our priorities.

Postscript to the Dialogue with the Gates Foundation

The Gates Foundation's response to this chapter was written by Stacey Childress and Irvin Scott in a post titled: *"The Role of the Marketplace in Education."*[219]

In their response, Irvin Scott offered the following assessment:

As I have reflected on these exchanges, my meeting with Mr. Cody here at the foundation, and my life's work as an educator with a deep commitment to equity and opportunity, I must agree with how Mr. Cody started his last column: we have different realities.

Simply, I believe all children can learn. I believe low-income children of color can learn when they have great teachers who believe in them, and treat them with the same passion, enthusiasm and intellectual rigor that they would treat their own children. And I believe in the skill and will of teachers, provided they are given the opportunity to teach, learn and lead as true professionals. I believe in John Dewey's insight that learning in the process of living is the deepest form of freedom. In a nation that aspires to democracy, that's what education is primarily for: the cultivation of freedom within society.

I want to believe that Mr. Cody believes this same truth about students, yet in each post he carefully marshals an assortment of facts and statistics which seems to suggest that he believes that children living in poverty cannot learn and that until the status quo changes we should lower our expectations for poor children.

This represents the basic indictment that was issued against educators by George W. Bush when he launched *No Child Left Behind*. According to this portrayal, teachers like me are guilty of subjecting our students to the "soft bigotry of low expectations."

I am not sure where in my work I have ever expressed the idea that poor children cannot learn, but apparently my repeated efforts to document the real effects of poverty carried that message for Mr. Scott.

The public dialogue with the Gates Foundation ended with this chapter and the Gates Foundation's response. I arranged for Mr. Scott to visit New Highland Academy in the fall of 2013 to witness firsthand the teacher inquiry work there. He spent the afternoon observing and discussing the work with teachers and researchers from Mills College, but he has not returned to follow up on that experience.

Part III

Gates' Education Dystopia

We don't have 50 different kinds of electrical sockets—we have just one. And that standard unleashed all kinds of innovation that improved lives. The same thing will happen with consistent standards for what students should know.

Bill Gates, 2014[220]

How can this regime of precise measurement and of panoptical managerial vision be transferred to a context where the objects of production are the treatment of sick patients, the transactions between teachers and pupils, or decisions to hire and fire employees? The answer is that the structure and context of these activities must be expressed in a form that can be captured by the system, so that their digital representations can then be read and analyzed.

Simon Head, 2014[221]

Bill Gates is both an engineer and an entrepreneur. He looks at our educational system from the dual lens of an engineer who wants the pieces of this complex system to work together, and from the point of view of a technological entrepreneur, who wants to make the system as open as possible to all sorts of technologically based learning systems. Innovation is described in glowing terms as arriving when the educational marketplace has been opened up, when we have common standards across all fifty states. Innovation is not the domain of teachers or students, but of those who are creating the next generation of digital devices.

As a classroom teacher, I enjoyed bringing new technology to my students – whether it was a laserdisc player, computers, or digital video cameras. But these devices were never more than tools. In the educational future Gates is attempting to bring to us, technology has a far more powerful role – one I believe must be questioned.

Chapter 15

Wiring Our Students With Galvanic Response Bracelets?

"We are technocrats," Bill Gates stated in 2012.[222] What do technocrats believe and do? They think that technology and science provide the answers for the problems we face. Our educational system is today being rewired by technocrats such as Gates.

What might the future look like in this technologically driven education system?

Teachers and students may be fitted with "Galvanic Response Bracelets," which are described this way:

> The Affectiva Q Sensor is a wearable, wireless biosensor that measures emotional arousal via skin conductance, a form of electrodermal activity that grows higher during states such as excitement, attention or anxiety and lower during states such as boredom or relaxation.[223]

Researchers at Clemson University received a grant from the Gates Foundation for the following:

> Purpose: to work with members of the Measuring Effective Teachers (MET) team to measure engagement physiologically with Galvanic Skin Response (GSR) bracelets which will determine the feasibility and utility of using such devices regularly in schools with students and teachers.

> Amount: $498,055[224]

Yet another, even larger grant, went to the *National Center on Time and Learning*:

> Purpose: to measure engagement physiologically with Functional Magnetic Resonance Imaging and Galvanic Skin Response to determine correlations between each measure and develop a scale that differentiates different degrees or levels of engagement.

> Amount: $621,265[225]

The Gates-funded *Measures of Effective Teaching* project has been experimenting with placing video cameras in classrooms for purposes of teacher evaluation. Currently the cameras are there only four times a year, for specific lessons. But some people are suggesting cameras be present constantly, like the dashboard cameras on a highway patrol car.[226] *MET* project leader Tom Kane said "That right now for us is a bridge too far."[227] But just as the creation of VAM systems for teacher evaluations led to those scores being published in newspapers, this is one cat that may be hard to keep in a bag. What do you teachers have to hide, anyway?

When public concerns were raised about the use of these bracelets, the Gates Foundation said that there had been a mistake, and that they never intended them to be used for evaluating teachers. A report in Forbes states:

> The biometric bracelets were not supposed to measure teachers' effectiveness, insisted Deborah Veney Robinson, the foundation's senior communications officer. The grants are not related to the Measures of Effective Teaching research project, and "will not in any way be used to evaluate teacher performance."

> So what are these bracelets for? According to the foundation, they are intended to "help students and teachers gain a better understanding of how and when students are most engaged in the classroom."[228]

But whether used for formal teacher evaluations, or simply as a means of monitoring student attentiveness, the use of these bracelets is intrusive. I do not share the faith Bill Gates and his foundation place in the capacity of technology to transform all aspects of education. There are, of course, marvelous ways technology can be used to allow students to communicate and create, and allow teachers to work with students in all sorts of new ways. But at the heart of learning is the connection and transmission of ideas, emotions, empathy and information between human beings. The wonderful thing about having human beings as teachers is that we are naturally empathetic. We do not need galvanic skin sensors to detect when our students are drowsy or disinterested -- we can look around the room in an instant and know! We need to honor and enhance this human capacity, rather than seek mechanical devices that clumsily attempt to replicate it.

Videotaping lessons is not without value - and can be a useful way to reflect on our practice. But the idea of using cameras to monitor instruction over the course of the year, especially when combined with an increasingly rigid and specific set of instructional and curricular guidelines, is frightening. If teacher evaluation is about us reflecting and learning about how we can better reach all our students, it is a wonderful thing. If it becomes an exercise in constantly monitoring instruction to ensure compliance with district mandates, it is a dagger in the heart of good teaching.

These systems have a way of growing on their own accord, especially when companies that produce them lobby heavily for their adoption. The Gates Foundation ought to consider the limitations and potential dangers of technology, as well as the potential benefits. As the Jeff Goldblum character in Jurassic Park remarks, "...your scientists were so preoccupied with whether or not they could, they didn't stop to think if they should."

Chapter 16

Bill Gates' TED Talk: Are Video Cameras the Missing Link?

I watched Bill Gates' May, 2013 *TED* Talk, to hear him explain why we should spend $5 billion to put video cameras in every classroom in the nation. But before I get to what he said, I want to share some of the wisdom that preceded him.

Rita Pierson starts us off with a bang, speaking of how human relationships are the prerequisite for learning:

> Kids don't learn from people they don't like. Apologize... Tell the kids you're sorry – they're in shock... We listen to policy that doesn't make sense, and we teach anyway. Teaching and learning should bring joy. How powerful would our world be if we had kids who were not afraid to take risks, and who had a champion? Every child deserves a champion, an adult who will never give up on them, and insists that they become the best that they can be.[229]

Teacher Ramsey Musallam shows how he provokes students to ask questions, and allows curiosity to drive their inquiries:

> If we, as educators, leave behind the simple role as disseminators of content, and embrace a new paradigm, as cultivators of curiosity and inquiry, we just might bring a little more meaning to their school day, and spark their imagination.[230]

16 year old student Shahruz Ghaemi says:

An administrative culture that focuses on standardized testing does us no good at all, because there is a difference between knowledge and understanding... If you truly understand something, it's far more important to you, it's more likely to be retained, it's far more likely to have some sort of meaning to you.[231]

So now we come to Bill Gates, and his $5 billion idea.

First, his rationale:

... there's one group of people that get almost no systematic feedback to help them do their jobs better. Until recently, 98% of teachers just got one word of feedback: 'satisfactory.' Today, districts are revamping the way they evaluate teachers. But we still give them almost no feedback that actually helps them improve their practice. Our teachers deserve better. The system we have today isn't fair to them. It's not fair to students, and it's putting America's global leadership at risk.[232]

Do you notice something? He starts out talking about feedback, but then slides into describing a formal evaluation process. There are LOTS of ways to enhance feedback that could have nothing at all to do with evaluation "systems" -- which, thanks to the determined and well-funded advocacy of the Gates Foundation and its projects, has already been redirected towards test scores and VAMs.

Next, he offers us the familiar international rankings, which find the US somewhere in the middle. Of the top performers, he ignores #3, Finland, in order to focus on Shanghai:

Let's look at the best academic performer, the province of Shanghai, China. Now, they rank #1 across the board, in reading, math and science. And one of the keys to Shanghai's success is the way they help teachers keep improving. They have weekly study groups, where teachers get together and talk about what's working. They even require each teacher to observe, and give feedback, to their colleagues. You might ask, 'why is a system like this so important?' It's because there's so much variation in the teaching profession. Some teachers are far more effective than others. In fact there are teachers throughout the country who are helping their students make extraordinary gains. If today's average teacher could become as good as those teachers, our students would be blowing away the rest of the world. So we need a system that helps all our teachers be as good as the best.

This raises so many more questions than it answers. How are teachers in Shanghai reflecting on their teaching? What guides them? Their system is reputed to focus on test preparation. How do we know the students are better prepared for their adult lives - beyond test scores?

Yong Zhao has written:

...what brings great test scores may hamper entrepreneurial qualities. Standardized testing and a focus on rote memorization, for example, are perhaps the biggest enemies of entrepreneurial capability.[233]

Gates goes on in his *TED* Talk to suggest that his foundation's *MET* project has found the solution:

We had observers watch videos of teachers in the classroom, and rate how they did on a range of practices. For example, did they ask their students challenging questions? Did they find multiple ways to explain an idea? We also had students fill out surveys, with questions like 'does your teacher know when the class understands a lesson?' 'Do you learn to correct your mistakes?' And what we found is very exciting. First, the teachers who did well on these observations had far better student outcomes. So it tells us we're asking the right questions. And second, teachers in the program told us that these videos and these surveys from the students were very helpful diagnostic tools, because they pointed to specific places where they can improve.

Once again, as we know from our previous experience with the Gates Foundation's work, "student outcomes" is a euphemism for test scores.

I want to draw on the wisdom shared at the beginning of this chapter by educator Ruth Pierson, who passed away in June, 2013, shortly after her *TED* Talk was recorded. Pierson spoke of the power of relationships in learning. Surely this is true for our growth as teachers as much as it is for our students? It is truly amazing to me that in proposing that we devise new ways for teachers to gain feedback, Bill Gates has focused his attention on investing in a device, rather than a learning process.

Video can be useful, and if any teacher in the US wants to record a lesson, I bet you they could find a smart phone or camcorder able to do the job. But why do we need video to observe one another? Even the teachers in Shanghai apparently are observing one another directly. The teachers in a given school are familiar with their context and students, and are well equipped to offer one another feedback, given time and support. This work builds on the trusting relationships between peers, who are devoted to bringing out the best in each other. We could call it *Lesson Study* - and learn from people who have been doing this kind of work for the past two decades.[234] We could engage in teacher inquiry, as we have seen groups like the Mills Teacher Scholars model for us.[235]

Linda Darling-Hammond recently pointed out that, in line with Bill Gates' main point, often teachers do not have the opportunities to provide feedback to each other. But Darling-Hammond does not suggest that the lack of video cameras is the culprit. Rather, she writes:

> ...evidence suggests that time afforded to educators to collaborate and problem-solve is eroding quickly. As recently as 2009, a MetLife study indicated that 68% of educators had more than an hour per week to engage in structured collaboration with colleagues to improve student learning. By 2012, only 48% had an hour or more per week for this essential work. In what professional field can practice improve if most practitioners don't have even an hour a week to work together collaboratively?[236]

Bill Gates has described himself as a technocrat, so perhaps it is natural that he would fixate on some piece of technology as the missing element. But the real things that are missing are providing time for teachers to work together, and an understanding that this time will be most fruitful when teachers are given the autonomy to tackle the challenges they face, rather than being micromanaged and driven by test score data.

Sir Ken Robinson, one of the most famous TED talkers of all, closed out the show. He reminds us of some things that, if Bill Gates were listening, might serve as valuable feedback for him:

Education, under *No Child Left Behind*, is based on - not diversity, but conformity. What schools are encouraged to do is find out what kids can do across a very narrow spectrum of achievement. One of the effects of *NCLB* has been to narrow the curriculum to those areas that are tested, and what we've heard here... is that kids prosper best with a broad and diverse curriculum.

Right beneath the surface are these seeds of possibility, waiting for the right conditions to come about. You take an area, a school, a district, you change the conditions, give people a different sense of possibility, a different set of expectations, a broader range of opportunities, you cherish and value the relationships between teachers and learners, you offer people discretion to be creative and to innovate in what they do, and schools that were once bereft spring to life.

The real role of leadership in education, at the national level, the state level and the school level, is not and should not be "command and control." The real role of leadership is climate control. Creating a climate of possibility. And if you do that, people will rise to it, and achieve things that you did not anticipate and couldn't have expected.[237]

For some reason, all this feedback has escaped Bill Gates. If only he had a video camera.

Chapter 17

Dystopia: A Possible Future of Teacher Evaluation

Picture our public schools in the year 2018. What follows is an attempt to see a few short years into the future, to understand how current reform proposals may develop.

I have been skeptical about the proposals from the Gates Foundation regarding teacher evaluation, because they do not correspond with how I have seen teachers collaborate and grow together. There is the language of feedback and growth, but I am fearful of a dystopian outline I see emerging, driven by Gates' technocratic vision. The "system" has been described in vague terms - elements of student and parent feedback, teacher observations, videotapes - and a $5 billion price tag. To offer some perspective, assuming there are five million classrooms in America, that amounts to about $1000 per classroom. What is all this money going to buy?

I want to describe the possible future I see. Am I wrong to be uneasy or even fearful of this? Here is the outline I find a bit scary.

The year is 2018. We have a national system of standards, curriculum, technological enhancements and high stakes tests, all aligned and built out as described by Bill Gates in 2009.[238] Teachers arrive at school and are handed not just the keys to the classroom, but the whole year's curriculum, which has been developed by "experts" and "innovators" - meaning textbook publishers and educational software developers. There is an optimum way to deliver each lesson, as has been determined by field testing, and teachers are told to watch a video to ensure they know how it ought to be delivered.

There is a detailed timeline, to make sure that students cover all the material required for each grade level, so they stay on track for college and career. Much of the instruction is done online, in large "flipped" classrooms. "Personalization" is achieved by having each student work autonomously, using educational software, taking periodic assessments to track their progress. Student essays are uploaded to automated scoring systems, which quickly and efficiently return detailed feedback on punctuation and sentence structure, but offer no capacity for understanding what the student has attempted to communicate. Teachers become managers of this interface between students and the standardized curriculum.

There are computer-based benchmark tests aligned with the curriculum every six weeks, to make sure the teacher is covering the material according to the timeline. Then there is an end of year test that covers all the material learned, and this allows the student to receive credit for course completion. The teacher is also given credit for the material the students have learned. Teachers and students have unique ID numbers that are attached to all their records. Both student and teacher data are stored in a data warehouse, which is made available to school districts, colleges, and companies doing various forms of research and product development.

Each classroom has its own video camera. These cameras are networked and controlled from the school or district office. Teachers are directed to record lessons of particular topics, which are coded according to the standards that are addressed. Then when the test scores arrive, teachers who have students that have performed above expectations on their tests have their videos placed in a "preferred practices" library for reference by teachers and evaluators. Teachers whose students perform consistently below expectations are flagged for more intensive review and feedback, or fired, depending on their status and level of due process protection.

Since principals do not have sufficient time to observe and supervise teachers, this work is contracted out to "experts," (hired by for-profit service providers) who are sent the videos to review remotely. They provide a summary of what they observe, using as their guideline the checklist of best practices and the instructions for that particular lesson. This is included in the teachers' evaluation.

Teachers are provided with this feedback, and given the chance to improve - they can review the videos of more effective teachers, and work to deliver their lessons according to the script or best practices guidelines. These key lessons are once again delivered, videotaped, and the teachers are scored on their performance.

Teachers who fail to respond to this feedback, and whose students continue to perform poorly on assessments, are fired. This system uses the following "multiple measures" of data to ensure that it is an accurate representation of a teachers' effectiveness:

- Video of the teacher engaged in instruction, scored by experts.

- Student test scores and VAM analyses.

- Student and parent survey data.

- Principal's observations.

The comprehensive data system will contain a complete record of each teacher's performance. If any school district is contemplating hiring a teacher, they will enter the teacher's code number and access all this information.

This is a future I believe is possible given the systems and structures being promoted by technocrats like Gates. This is NOT the way the system has been described by Bill Gates or any of his representatives. They tend to use the language of feedback and collaboration. But as I have been asking, if collaboration is the goal, why must this be embedded in an evaluation process, which has the goal of determining who ought to be fired?

Teachers are already being evaluated based on the test scores of students they never taught. Every subject is being assigned some form of standardized test, so that student and teacher performance can be quantified and compared.

Measurement has already run amok, and the plans we are seeing outlined expand this dramatically. In this climate, I believe more collection of data allows for more inappropriate uses of data, and we are far beyond the place where this data is helping.

If I thought that creating this ultimate system of alignment would result in better lives for students, I would get with the program. However, we know that high stakes tests are far more effective at reinforcing inequities than breaking them down. Students are not standardized, and teachers do their best work when they can teach creatively, building on student interests, and responding to their needs. Conformity and standardization may create efficient marketplaces, but they will drive the vitality from our classrooms.

If I am wrong, and the new evaluation system described by Bill Gates really is all about feedback and collaboration, then why not remove the model from an evaluative framework? Make the sharing of videos voluntary and low-stakes. Provide teachers dedicated time for collaboration. Offer a variety of structures such as Lesson Study, Critical Friends and Teacher Inquiry, that have been proven effective at generating authentic reflection and growth.

If I turn out to be right, then smash the cameras, boycott the tests, opt out of the data systems, and refuse to be standardized and scripted.

Chapter 18

Are Education Innovators Channeling B.F. Skinner?

Phil McCrae has written a fascinating history of "innovation" in education that should be required reading for everyone.[239] As I was reading this account, I clicked on the video the author embedded. This grainy film from 1954 features B.F. Skinner, describing the virtues of the "teaching machine." Here are Skinner's words:

> With this machine, the student sees a bit of text or other printed material. As soon as the student has finished his response he operates the machine and learns immediately whether he was right or wrong. This is a great improvement over the system in which papers are corrected by a teacher, where the student must wait, perhaps til another day, to learn whether or not what he has written is right. Such immediate knowledge has two principle effects. It leads most rapidly to the formation of correct behavior. The student quickly learns to be right. But there is also a motivating effect. The student is free of uncertainty or anxiety about his success or failure. His work is pleasurable. He does not have to force himself to study. A classroom in which machines are being used is usually the scene of intense concentration.

> One function of the teaching machine then is to give the student a quick report on the adequacy of his response. This is important not only for efficient learning - it generates a high level of interest and enthusiasm.

Another important advantage is that the student is free to move at his own pace. With techniques in which a whole class is forced to move forward together, the bright student wastes time waiting for others to catch up. And the slow student, who may not be inferior in any other respect, is forced to go too fast.

A third feature of machine teaching is that each student follows a carefully constructed program, leading from the initial stage where he is wholly unfamiliar with the subject, to a final stage in which he is competent. He does this by taking a large number of very small steps, arranged in a coherent order.... Programs have been constructed in which, without any prior study, the student is right 95% of the time. This is partly due to the fact that the student only moves on when he has completely mastered all the preceding material.

A conservative estimate seems to be that with these machines, the average grade school or high school student can cover about twice as much material with the same amount of time and effort as with traditional classroom techniques.

There is no magic about this. A teaching machine is simply a convenient way of bringing the student into contact with the man who writes the program. It is the author of the program, not the machine, who teaches. He and the student are constantly interacting.[240]

What is remarkable in listening to Dr. Skinner is how familiar these promises seem. Here, 60 years ago, we have the promise that students can work at their own pace, through curriculum presented in a coherent order by a "teaching machine". The student interacts constantly with the author of the machine's program, and the result is that learning proceeds twice as fast. The word "personalized" is the only thing missing - but the idea is there for sure.

So what is wrong with these machines and this mechanical "personalization"? The modern versions of such teaching machines are certainly more sophisticated than these dinosaurs of the 1950s. But they have more in common than just the promises made on their behalf.

If we look over the shoulders of children in computer labs today, most of the programs are variations of those described by Dr. Skinner.

Students are given a short text or math problem and must provide the correct answer. Often there is a game or snazzy cartoon characters to dress up the process and make it more fun, but the essence has not changed much. Students follow a course of study with bits of learning sprinkled along a pathway, and then take periodic tests to show they have mastered that mouthful.

As Phil McCrae points out, a vision very reminiscent of Skinner's continues to drive national education policy today.

The U.S. Department of Education (2013) has clearly articulated a commitment to making this happen with 'Competency-Based Learning' or 'Personalized Learning':

> Transitioning away from seat time, in favor of a structure that creates flexibility, allows students to progress as they demonstrate mastery of academic content, regardless of time, place, or pace of learning. By enabling students to master skills at their own pace, competency-based learning systems help to save both time and money...make better use of technology, support new staffing patterns that utilize teacher skills and interests differently...Each of these presents an opportunity to achieve greater efficiency and increase productivity. [241]

Even more sophisticated machines are on the way, which will analyze and assess student essays, using algorithms that look at the vocabulary and sentence structure to determine if students are writing well.[242] But these systems do not understand the real meaning the writer is attempting to convey. That means that you can score high with sentences that are written with proper grammar, using advanced vocabulary, but be expressing absolute nonsense. Les Perelman has done extensive research that shows that computerized grading is a poor substitute for humans.[243]

Computers are, of course, useful tools. And they have a place in the classroom as well. But there are good reasons that in the decade following Dr. Skinner's unveiling of his teaching machine that they did not spread beyond a few lab schools.

Computers are the basis of the "competency-based learning systems" that are being sold to our schools, and which are also being used to measure student performance. Our education system is being engineered to produce student outcomes aligned with the new standards, and as we saw in the Seattle school system, those outcomes will be measured using computers.[244] This means we must be more mindful than ever of the limitations of computers. David Auerbach wrote:

> There is good news and bad news. The good news is that, because computers cannot and will not "understand" us the way we understand each other, they will not be able to take over the world and enslave us (at least not for a while). The bad news is that, because computers cannot come to us and meet us in our world, we must continue to adjust our world and bring ourselves to them. We will define and regiment our lives, including our social lives and our perceptions of our selves, in ways that are conducive to what a computer can 'understand.' Their dumbness will become ours.[245]

In a sense, this is where our obsession with the measurement of learning leads us as well. We can only manage what we can measure, we are told by our managers. So in order to improve the students who graduate from our schools, we must define learning in terms of measurable outcomes. As we shift to using computers to do this measurement for us, these outcomes are more and more defined by the ways computers can "understand" what our students can do.

For our students, this is not, by and large, an innovation that empowers. While computers can lead them through the steps to learn certain skills, there are places that only a good teacher can take them.

Students are highly social, and most learn best when they are together in a supportive classroom community. They have their own interests and curiosities, and they really get excited about learning when they have the chance to pursue them. They make meaning by connecting what they are learning to the real world. In April, 2013, David Greene posed the question for the *New York Times Dialogue*, "What makes a great teacher?" Part of his answer reads:

> Seasoned professionals know what works: being creative, independent, spontaneous, practical and rule-bending. Often it is the least orthodox teacher who most engages and excites students. Scripts and rules and models strictly followed cannot replace what the best teachers have:

practical wisdom.[246]

This aligns with what we are hearing from students as well. Also in April 2013, members of the *Providence Student Union* issued their own vision for education, which said in part:

> We're told to sit and listen, to do our test prep so we can pass our NECAP and move on. But that's not how we learn. That's certainly not how I learn. We need an education that is as creative as we are. We need projects, hands-on learning, debates, and conversations. We need opportunities to do arts and technology and to work in groups. And we need small enough classes where teachers have the flexibility to teach us like individuals.[247]

Students want computers they can use as tools to expand what they can create, not "teaching machines" with all the answers programmed into them. B.F. Skinner gave us an example of an innovative teaching machine that went nowhere. In order to avoid his mistakes, we need to look beyond the glamour of the new, to see if innovations can allow students to be truly creative.

Chapter 19

Are MOOCs Missing the Mark?

Some people have been very enthused about the potential for MOOCs - Massive Open Online Courses. In the summer of 2013, Bill Gates praised them for bringing us the "golden era" of learning.[248] Later that year, Bill Gates told community college leaders that they should embrace the trend. The *Chronicle for Higher Education* reported:

> As MOOC lectures evolve, the average classroom professor will have a hard time competing, and the traditional lecture will seem antiquated, Mr. Gates suggested.
>
> "The quality of those lectures, as they go through the competitive process, will be extremely good," he said. "No individual performance is likely to come up to that level."[249]

The Gates Foundation has invested millions[250] in supporting the development of a variety of MOOCs, but early results are less than encouraging. The experience may teach us some important lessons about how people learn - if we are willing to pay attention.

To be fair, Gates has acknowledged that there are issues and problems to be worked out. An October, 2013 report on the *Communications of the ACM* blog reveals what some of those issues are, and shows some rather worrisome results.[251]

Karen Head, a professor at the *Georgia Institute of Technology*, received Gates funding to offer a MOOC version of a freshman composition class.

Head reports:[252]

We had 21,934 students enrolled, 14,771 of whom were active in the course. Our 26 lecture videos were viewed 95,631 times. Students submitted work for evaluation 2,942 times and completed 19,571 peer assessments (the means by which their writing was evaluated). However, only 238 students received a completion certificate-- meaning that they completed all assignments and received satisfactory scores.

She offers some thoughts about why so few completed the course:

...For one thing, students who did not complete all three major assignments could not pass the course. Many struggled with technology, especially in the final assignment, in which they were asked to create a video presentation based on a personal philosophy or belief. Some students, for privacy and cultural reasons, chose not to complete that assignment, even when we changed the guidelines to require only an audio presentation with visual elements. There were other students who joined the course after the second week; we cautioned them that they would not be able to pass it because there was no mechanism for doing peer review after an assignment's due date had passed.

She also states, that while it was exciting to experiment with this approach:

...I don't think any of us (writing and communication instructors) would rush to teach another MOOC soon. For now, the technology is lacking for courses in subject areas like writing, which have such strong qualitative evaluation requirements. Too often we found our pedagogical choices hindered by the course-delivery platform we were required to use, when we felt that the platform should serve the pedagogical requirements. Too many decisions about platform functionality seem to be arbitrary, or made by people who may be excellent programmers but, I suspect, have never been teachers.

Gee whiz, I wonder who else that last line could describe?

According to the experiment just completed by Professor Head, the proportion of students who fit this model of learning is 238 out of 21,934 enrolled. Just over one percent. A graduate student who researched completion rates for 29 different MOOCs found the average rate was seven percent.[253]

I have my own hypothesis about the limitations we are discovering in the MOOCs, but first I have an observation about the model of learning to which Bill Gates seems to be drawn. We have heard from Gates for years about the great resource we would have if we could capture outstanding teachers lecturing on video. And he has invested millions in supporting the *Khan Academy*, which is an attempt to do just that. He often describes this as allowing for "personalization," in that the learner can watch the lecture videos at his own pace, and that this could free up the instructors to work with students one on one. But it does not seem to be working this way.

I think there may be a certain type of learner that this works for - someone who is highly motivated and purposeful, who is seeking out specific knowledge. And someone who does not require much human interaction - because in spite of the rhetoric about personalization, lectures are inherently impersonal, and videos of lectures are doubly so.

So if the MOOC is ushering in a golden age, democratizing access to knowledge, it seems to have hit a bit of an obstacle. I think the bump in the road is the learner.

California's San Jose State University has been experimenting with MOOCs through a partnership with *Udacity*. The University recently ended this project after finding lackluster results. One incident highlights one of the problems:

> After watching the ethics MOOC, taught by Harvard professor Michael Sandel, the San Jose philosophy faculty wrote an open letter in protest.[254] Hadreas says it would be insulting to force diverse state university students to watch the Ivy League professor lecture to his affluent class. "He would incorporate into his talks how privileged they were," Hadreas says. "They were for the most part more white than our student body. So we got on the one hand this strange upstairs-downstairs situation, where the lower-class people could

look at how the upper-class people were educated."[255]

Of course, some might assume that a Harvard professor is among the best in the world. And he may be - for his own students. But even in delivering a lecture, that Harvard professor is directly relating to the students in his presence. Students watching this lecture on video are beyond his awareness - he is not speaking directly to them. Though they can hear him, they are not with him. This is the complete opposite of personalization.

Great teachers know their students and make every effort to communicate on a personal level with them as individuals. They communicate not just information, but also concern, compassion and encouragement. They find ways to build students' confidence in their own abilities. They can intuit confusion in the room, and stop to explain or provide more context. They can draw students into active discussions, building on prior experiences and understanding. None of this is possible when those students watch a video recorded lesson.

For more than a century, public libraries have offered places where thousands of books are freely available to all. Libraries have democratized access to information. In a sense, the advent of the internet, and the videotaped lectures made available through MOOCs, are a new sort of library. This provides a resource available to many people. But just making information available is not the same as teaching. Libraries are wonderful, but they have not replaced schools. And for similar reasons, MOOCs are unlikely to replace in-person classes.

Chapter 20

The Classroom of the Future: Student-Centered or Device-Centered?

A basic question is emerging as our schools are urged to embrace the Common Core State Standards and the computer-based learning systems aligned to the standards. Are these digital devices becoming central to the classroom—and coming to dominate the way we teach and learn? And how will this serve our students?

In March, 2014 we heard from Bill Gates the virtues of the Common Core explained this way:

> "If you have 50 different plug types, appliances wouldn't be available and would be very expensive," he said. But once an electric outlet becomes standardized, many companies can design appliances and competition ensues, creating variety and better prices for consumers, he said.[256]

In the classroom, these "appliances" are the tablets and other digital devices now being aggressively sold. In 2012, Gates explained this model of device-centered "personalization":

> Teachers have not had these tools before. Fragmented standards that differ from state to state and district to district have made it hard for innovators to design tools to reach a wide market. The common core will help change that. In the classroom of the not-too-far-off future, kids will have computer devices with phenomenal interactive content. This will allow teachers to do what they call "flip the classroom."

Instead of learning a concept in class and applying it at home, students would learn the concept at home, on video, and apply it in class, where they can get help from the teacher. When students learn a concept on video, they can take as much time as they need and learn at their own pace. They can pause the video, rewind it, or just listen to it all over again. Then the students can use class time to do the problems. The teacher sees instantly on the dashboard which kids are getting it, and steps in if someone is stuck. The students move on when they master the material, and not before. This is very different from the old method where every student moves on to the next topic after the test, whether you got an A or a D.[257]

Iwan Streichenberger, the CEO of the now-defunct Gates-funded inBloom data-storage project used a slightly different analogy:

Our purpose is to remove the friction in the deployment of technology in the classroom. It's not very exciting, but if you don't have plumbing you can't have appliances.[258]

In (now defunct) inBloom's view, the "plumbing" is the system that will allow data from all these devices to be collected and used by all the appliance makers. Our classrooms are being re-wired and standardized to allow the proliferation of appliances that will transform education.

What do these appliances look like? What does this transformation entail?

At Austin's SXSWedu, in March of 2014, I attended the product launch for one such appliance. Rupert Murdoch's Amplify has produced a new tablet for the classroom market, which comes with a complete ELA, math, and science curriculum. The program promises:

With an e-library stocked with more than 300 books and educational games, and tools for immediate, in-class student assessment, Amplify ELA aims to help students read three times more and write three times more, and to help teachers provide three times more meaningful feedback.[259]

As the students work, the device keeps track of what they have read and written. Words that were misspelled are repeated on new assignments they are given. The teacher has an interface that allows them to monitor student work, and choose from a menu of pre-programmed feedback responses with a tap of a finger.

Another provider of "appliances" is Microsoft, which has partnered with Pearson to produce what they are calling the "*Common Core System of Courses*, with the Windows 8 touchscreen technology."

Margo Day, the vice president of U.S. Education, for Microsoft explains:

> Personalized learning for every student is a worthy and aspirational goal. By combining the power of touch, type, digital inking, multitasking and split-screen capabilities that Windows 8 with Office 365 provides with these new Pearson applications, we're one step closer to enabling an interactive and personalized learning environment.[260]

In this mode of instruction, these devices become the mediator of almost every academic interaction between students and their teacher, and even with one another. Students are assigned work on the device, they perform their work on the device, they share work through the device, and they receive feedback via the device. What is more, the means by which learning is measured—the standardized test—will also be via this device.

It is the appliance that now becomes "intelligent" about each student, and the appliance is the vehicle by which lessons are "personalized," because the appliance is keeping track of what the student is capable of, and where the student is weak.

Of course the teacher has the ability to oversee and monitor the assignments the device is making, but the whole idea is to automate this process. And this is happening in an environment where there is a clear desire to increase class sizes. Thus we have "personalization" via digital device, at the same time we make teacher-student relationships far more difficult because budget constraints are increasing class sizes.

The Rocketship charter schools have attempted to make this formula work, but thus far have not seen good results.[261]

Unfortunately, school finance has become a zero sum game, so that when Los Angeles Unified decided to invest a billion dollars in iPads and Pearson curriculum, that meant that this money was diverted from sorely needed facility renovation bond funds.[262]

I know from my many years teaching middle school that students LOVE new technology. I recall when we got laserdisc machines back in the 1990s. Students enjoyed playing *Science Sleuths* and using the barcode reader to find the answers.

But as enthusiastic as the laserdisc vendors were, their claims never reached the ambitions of the current generation of appliance peddlers. And I think these devices will fail ultimately fail to deliver. Here is why:

- Students are best motivated and engaged by teachers who have the time to give them individual attention.

- The most engaging lessons are not going to come from a device, programmed by Pearson pedagogues who have never met students. They are going to be developed by creative teachers building on the interests of their students.

- The initial excitement of using touchscreen tablets, and seeing little animations whiz around the printed words of a reading assignment is likely to wear off in a year or two, leaving students with an expensive portable textbook/workbook.

- Parents have become increasingly alarmed at the ability of these devices to capture vast amounts of highly detailed information about their children, and have mounted such opposition that the Gates-funded data storage giant inBloom was forced to close its doors.

- Teachers with manageable class sizes are far better at understanding and relating to the personal interests and abilities of their students than even the best device. Teachers have the added capability of interpersonal relationship - which no device has yet achieved. Thus, smaller class sizes remain a more prudent investment than devices which will be obsolete in a few years.[263]

- While the Amplify tablet boasts of more than "300 books and games," a good school library might house thousands of print books, allowing far more options for readers. There are also concerns as to the way the human brain interacts with a screen compared to the printed page.[264]

- The idea that educational improvement will be driven by innovations resulting from competition between these various designers of devices is based on a basic misunderstanding. Creativity and innovation have always been of greatest educational value when they emerge from the autonomy given to classroom teachers and students.

It is understandable why people who have made their fortunes on the transformation of commerce and industry through the almighty combination of computers, software, data and the internet would project a similar revolution in our schools. However, there is a fundamental difference between commerce and the classroom. Our students learn in a social environment in which human relationships remain central. A model which makes a device and not the teacher and student central to the learning process is flawed.

These devices have some value as tools, and I am not suggesting they be abandoned. I am suggesting that they are being greatly oversold, and the imperative to standardize our classrooms so they become uniform "sockets" that will allow these devices to readily plug in is misguided. We stand to lose far more from this stultifying standardization than these devices can ever provide.

Chapter 21

Is Common Core Creating the Code for a Computerized Education System?

Astronomer Stephen Hawking recently raised concerns about the threat artificial intelligence poses to human civilization.[265] But even if we are not all turned into drones by some super mind, major changes are afoot, revealing both a bright and dark side of the technologies we find so addictive.

As teachers, most of us are excited to see our students turned on by the latest technologies. Computers allow students to conduct research on the web, email experts for information, gather images and view videos from around the world. Students can use digital tools to create, rather than simply consume. Students can make their own podcasts, tutorials, or creative projects.

But technology has a darker side as well. In the book *Mindless: Why Smarter Machines are Making Dumber Humans*, Simon Head explores these dimensions of 21st century technology.[266] Head describes the ways in which computers are being used to reorganize and manage all sorts of aspects of life and commerce.

American society is now organized for the convenience and profitability of corporations, who, as Gilens and Page recently documented, hold sway over the political process.[267] Those corporations have discovered the extraordinary value of "Computer Business Systems" (CBSs), which allow all sorts of processes to be rendered more efficient. As I read Simon Head's description of the ways these systems work, I began to understand some of the imperatives driving 21st century education "reform":

> CBSs are amalgams of different technologies that are pulled together to perform highly complex tasks in the control and monitoring of businesses, including their employees. The technologies of the Internet are crucial to CBSs because they provide the foundation for computer networks that can link the workstation of every employee or group of employees within an organization.

> Products known as 'data warehouses' and 'data marts' are also critical to the CBS control regime. Data warehouses contain the gigantic quantities of information needed to store data in millions of transactions performed daily by tens of thousands of employees - the raw material of the system. Data marts "cleanse" and order this data so that it can be used to evaluate performance in real time and in line with matrices established by management. Once data warehouses and data marts are fused with the monitoring capabilities of CBSs, then the building blocks of a very powerful system of workplace control are in place.[268]

When we think of work being controlled and sped up, the image of a factory worker comes to mind. We see Charlie Chaplin, in *Modern Times*, struggling to keep up with his assembly line. This movement for efficiency was called Taylorism, and transformed industrial production.[269] In the 21st century, this is not just for factory workers.

The way this works is that system designers develop rules that govern interactions between the different parts of a process - even when those parts are actually human beings. Then those processes are analyzed and the system is reorganized and optimized for efficiency. If you have interacted with telephone tech support, you may have experienced this sort of management. Our medical services are now being organized on this basis, with insurance providers who have very specific ideas about what "best practice" means - and it is usually that which is the fastest and costs the least.

Simon Head explains:

> How can this regime of precise measurement and of panoptic managerial vision be transferred to a context where the objects of

production are the treatment of sick patients, the transactions between teachers and pupils, or the decisions to hire and fire employees? The answer is that the structure and context of these activities must be expressed in a form that can be captured by the system, so that their digital representations can then be read analyzed. But the limits of 'capturability' become apparent when one looks at transactions between human agents where attempts to impose 'capturability,' and with it the disciplines of CBSs, distort the meaning of what is being done and leave the data generated highly vulnerable to GIGO - garbage in, garbage out.

So, what would be Gates' approach be to bringing this sort of efficient management to education?

First of all, we would need a discrete set of measurable learning objectives, such as the Common Core, that everyone agreed would be the goal for the K-12 system.

Next, we would need curriculum, and most importantly closely aligned tests, that would tell us if students had met these learning objectives.

Then we would need devices for students to work on that were capable of recording and transmitting their every keystroke, their every written thought, and everything they had read or viewed on their screen.

Finally, we would need data systems to track the performance of all the parts in the system. We would want to know how the students were doing, but we would also want to measure the effects of various learning technologies, readings, assignments and, of course, the effects of their teachers. So we would need systems to record, store, and analyze all this data.

Not sure how this would be possible? Take a minute to listen to Jose Ferreira, of Knewton:

Education happens to be the world's most data minable industry by far. And it's not even close.... The name of the game is data per user. So one of the things that fakes us out about data in education is because it is so big - like the fourth biggest industry in the world - it produces incredible quantities of data. But data that just produces one or two data points per user per day is not really all that valuable to an individual user. It might be valuable to like a school district administrator, but maybe not even then. So let's just compare. Netflix and Amazon get in the ones of data points per user per day. Google and Facebook get in the tens of data points per user per day. So you do ten minutes of messing around in Google and you produce about a dozen data points for Google. So Knewton today gets five to ten million actionable data points per student per day. Now we do that, because we get people, if you can believe it, to tag every single sentence of their content - we have a large publishing partnership with Pearson, and they've tagged all of their content. And we're an open standard, so anyone can tag to us. If you tag all of your content, and you do it down to the atomic concept level, down to the sentence, down to the clause, you unlock an incredible amount of trapped, hidden data.

We literally know everything about you and how you learn best. Everything. Because we have five orders of magnitude more data about you than Google has. We literally have more data about our students than any company has about anybody else, about anything, and it's not even close. That's how we do it.[270]

So this "learning system," according to Mr. Ferreira, can use its predictive power to know how to teach every concept to every student. And it is critical that all the students be connected, because the system draws its intelligence from its ability to analyze these trillions of data points from millions of students. Mr. Ferreira, in his 2012 speech above, claimed that in the following year his company would have the data for ten million students, and not long after that, 100 million.

Clearly you do not need teachers in this scenario, except perhaps to supervise the students as they work on their devices. Class sizes can expand significantly. You do not even need schools. All a student needs is some sort of computer and a connection to the internet.

This system to reorganize education sounds remarkably close to what Bill Gates has been advocating for the past few years. The Common Core would provide us with the list of discrete learning objectives; Pearson,

Amplify and various other tech companies are producing the devices, tagging their content to the standards. The Department of Education is funding the standards-aligned tests, to be taken on computers. The Gates Foundation created inBloom to function as the data warehouse, and though that entity has folded, the data collection has not stopped.

Gates spoke with teachers in March 2014:

If states use common academic standards, the quality of classroom materials and professional development will improve, Gates said. Much of that material will be digital tools that are personalized to the student, he said. "To get this innovation out, common standards will be helpful."[271]

The wave of technology that has transformed the US economy since the advent of the internet twenty years ago has yielded tremendous advances in efficiency and productivity. However, the benefits of these advances have flowed up to the top one percent - or even the top 0.1 percent. A September, 2013 report suggests that nearly half the jobs in the US may be lost in the next twenty years as a result of computerization.[272]

The people running the economy are looking for ways to cut any labor that can be rendered obsolete through technology, and educators are not immune to this trend.

The skills and abilities that students develop in school, under the guidance of skilled educators, are not so easily measured, and this is a powerful reason to reject the mechanization of education. The late Gerald Bracey offered this list of things not measured by tests:

- creativity
- critical thinking
- resilience
- motivation
- persistence
- curiosity
- endurance

- reliability

- enthusiasm

- empathy

- self-awareness

- self-discipline

- leadership

- civic-mindedness

- courage

- compassion

- resourcefulness

- sense of beauty

- sense of wonder

- honesty

- integrity

In the years to come, we can choose to conform to the most efficient ways to organize our work and the process of education, so as to cost the least amount possible, while delivering the technical skills required by the employers who still require human labor. Or we can flip the paradigm, and organize our schools and our lives to serve the full development of children as human beings. This choice transcends education, and runs through every aspect of our culture. It is a challenge that requires not the efficient calculations of a thinking machine, but the slower contemplation of a moral mind.

Part IV

Accountability for Gates?

One of the saddest lessons of history is this: If we've been bamboozled long enough, we tend to reject any evidence of the bamboozle. We're no longer interested in finding out the truth. The bamboozle has captured us. It's simply too painful to acknowledge, even to ourselves, that we've been taken. Once you give a charlatan power over you, you almost never get it back.

Carl Sagan, 1997[273]

The Gates Foundation's education reforms revolve around various forms of "accountability." Hold schools, administrators, teachers and students accountable for test scores, measure performance often, and use the resulting data to deliver consequences. But this accountability seems to only flow downward, and Gates and his acolytes have appointed themselves the all-powerful role of determining what is to be measured, and how. In the chapters that follow, I look upward through the magnifying lens that is upon us, and suggest that Gates himself be held accountable as well.

Chapter 22

Bill Gates and the Cult of Measurement: Efficiency Without Excellence

Bill Gates' annual Foundation letter for 2013 provides us with a reminder of the outlook guiding his philanthropic spending in education and other arenas.[274]

A preview of his letter stated this:

This year, my letter focuses on the catalytic role that measurement can play in reducing hunger, poverty, and disease. Setting goals and measuring progress are obviously not new ideas. But over the last year, I've really been struck by the impact this can have improving the lives of the poorest.[275]

Measurement has been central to the Gates vision for improving schools in the US as well. But this approach has not, in my view, improved the lives of the poorest among our students.

Ever since the passage of *No Child Left Behind* in 2001, school reform has been driven by measurement and numerical goals. But unfortunately for the poor, we are not measuring what matters most, nor are our responses to the measurements truly helpful.

Mathematician Cathy O'Neil has offered an interesting critique of the Gates method of solutions via measurement. She writes:

...the person who defines the model defines success, and by obscuring this power behind a data collection process and incrementally improved model results, it seems somehow sanitized and objective when it's not. Don't be fooled by the mathematical imprimatur: behind every model and every data set is a political process that chose that data and built that model and defined success for that model.[276]

There is an old saying, "when your only tool is a hammer, everything looks like a nail." In our schools, standardized tests are our hammers, and as Cathy O'Neil points out, the standards and the tests that measure what has been learned have lots of questionable assumptions built in.

In his letter, Bill Gates draws an appealing portrait of how teaching is being improved at Eagle Valley High School in Vail, Colorado. Reflecting on the findings of the Gates Foundation's *Measures of Effective Teaching* project, he points out that they focus on "several measures that schools should use to assess teacher performance, including test data, student surveys and assessments by trained evaluators."

Unfortunately, a closer look at their research shows that the way these various models are validated is by the degree to which they align with test scores. Gary Rubinstein has dug into the data available from Eagle Valley High. He concludes, "Perhaps there still is a miracle district out there proving that these reforms are working, but as far as I can tell Eagle County, Colorado isn't it."[277]

We could choose to measure other things, of course. The idea of measurement is not useless. The trouble is that some of the things we truly value are harder to measure, and so we devolve back to the simplest metrics - test scores. This is defined as the "outcome" that we desire. But this is only one of a host of outcomes that we actually want for our students.

Nothing makes this clearer than the personal decisions made by people with the MOST control over their own children's education. The schools attended by the very wealthy are not chosen for their test scores - in fact many of them do not give standardized tests at all. Neither do they use student test scores to evaluate their teachers.

While Bill Gates undoubtedly used test score data as the basis for his assertion that class size does not matter much, and should be allowed to rise, it is fair to assume that the small class sizes at the private school attended by his children offer outcomes other than test scores.

What are the outcomes these schools offer?

The Sidwell Friends School, attended by Sasha and Malia Obama, says this on their website:

> We cultivate in all members of our community high personal expectations and integrity, respect for consensus, and an understanding of how diversity enriches us, why stewardship of the natural world matters and why service to others enhances life. Above all, we seek to be a school that nurtures a genuine love of learning and teaches students 'to let their lives speak.'[278]

The Lakeside School, attended by Bill Gates himself several decades ago, and now by his children, says this:

> Lakeside's 5th- to 12th-grade student-centered academic program focuses on the relationships between talented students and capable and caring teachers. We develop and nurture students' passions and abilities and ensure every student feels known.
>
> Each student's curiosities and capabilities lead them to unique academic challenges that are sustained through a culture of support and encouragement. All students will find opportunities to discover and develop a passion; to hone the skills of writing, thinking, and speaking; and to interact with the world both on and off campus. Lakeside trusts that each student has effective ideas about how to maximize his or her own education, and that they will positively contribute to our vibrant learning community.[279]

The parents who send their children to these schools keep a sharp eye on the outcomes that really matter. They know that personal relationships are key, and that is something that cannot be measured on a test. It is something that is made possible by small class sizes and a warm environment that recognizes the uniqueness of every child.

This is the very opposite of using standardized measurement tools to score and rank every learner, and every teacher.

Back in 1947, Martin Luther King, Jr. wrote:

> The function of education, therefore, is to teach one to think intensively and to think critically. But education which stops with efficiency may prove the greatest menace to society.[280]

Measurement and standardization delivers efficiency without excellence. When this becomes the driving force in a marketized education system, it both fosters conformity and channels innovation towards commercially viable solutions for those unable to purchase the sort of personalized education the wealthy choose for their own children. Measurement in education will not serve the poor. It will merely make the schools attended by the poor more efficient in preserving their poverty.

Chapter 23

Bill Gates, Why Not Measure This?

In the previous chapter, I pointed out that Bill Gates apparently uses a different set of outcomes in choosing a school for his own children than the measurable ones his foundation advocates for the children of the less fortunate.

There are many outcomes that we value that are difficult to measure, leading to the first order of bias here, towards outcomes that are easily quantified. But there is a second order of bias at work - deliberate choices that are made to define the parameters of the system within which we measure.

Bill Gates wrote in his 2013 annual letter:

Given a goal, you decide on what key variable you need to change to achieve it-the same way a business picks objectives for inside the company like customer satisfaction-and develop a plan for change and a way of measuring the change. You use the measurement as feedback to make adjustments. I think a lot of efforts fail because they don't focus on the right measure or they don't invest enough in doing it accurately.[281]

The Gates Foundation has decided that the variable we can most readily change is the effectiveness of the classroom teacher. Therefore all their powers of measurement have focused on this single variable. We have explored in earlier chapters some of the problems with this. In particular, the fact that less than 20% of the differences in student growth can be attributed to their teacher suggests that perhaps we ought to be looking in the realm of the out of school factors, which have been found to account for more than 60% of these differences. In this chapter, I want to explore some of the areas that have remained unexamined.

What are some other things affecting our students that we should be measuring?

Here are some other things even more directly related to our children's performance in school and success in life beyond that could be measured, and improved. The first two are suggestions offered in this report: *Ten Ways to Promote Educational Achievement and Attainment Beyond the Classroom:*[282]

Measure the number of Unplanned Pregnancies:

The report tells us:

Research conducted in Europe has found that children and teens born as a result of unwanted pregnancies tend to receive poorer grades and ratings from teachers in early childhood and adolescence.

We could address this through effective sex education and contraception. Also:

Intensive early childhood programs that promote child well-being have also been effective at lowering unintended pregnancy and birth rates among program participants more than a decade later, when they have entered the teen years. Similarly, programs geared towards the health and well-being of low- income first-time mothers have been found to be effective at preventing subsequent unintended pregnancies.

Measure the availability of Prenatal Care:

We also learn that:

Research has found that maternal health in both the prenatal and early childhood stages has substantial effects on early childhood academic and cognitive outcomes. Mothers who smoke cigarettes, drink alcohol in excess, or use drugs during pregnancy are at risk of having children who display relatively poor cognitive abilities in math and English during the elementary school years. Mothers who have insufficient prenatal care may also be at risk of having children with poor early childhood cognitive and language skills.

Measure the level of funding available to each school district:

Per pupil funding can vary significantly, even within a single state or region.[283] And often the neediest students are the ones that receive the least support.

Measure the level of access to college:

The Gates Foundation has made it clear that, in their view, the primary purpose of a K12 education is to prepare students for college. However, in the past 30 years, the cost of attending a four year school has increased at four times the rate of inflation.[284]

College debt recently passed the trillion dollar mark, eclipsing the total amount Americans owe on credit cards.[285] This has prompted some to even suggest there may be a sort of bubble forming regarding the value of a college education. This puts college out of reach for many students, especially those lacking family wealth to back them up. It will do impoverished students little good to prepare them for college if they do not have the resources to stay and graduate, as was illustrated by this story in the *New York Times*.[286]

Measure the levels of childhood poverty, neighborhood violence, homelessness, and family members incarcerated:

All four of those factors have huge impacts on children's lives, directly affecting their future prospects.

Measure economic and racial segregation:

Research shows that underprivileged students do best when not highly concentrated. The greatest advances in student achievement occurred during the years when the US expanded desegregation programs. Unfortunately this is now being reversed -- and some advocates of charter schools are even suggesting this is a good thing.

Ken Bernstein suggests we measure exposure to lead:

Test all low-income children EARLY for lead - Michael Martin of the Arizona School Board Association has been pointing out the dangers of lead for years, and recently Kevin Drum has written on this.[287] While in theory public housing "remediated" lead-based paint, in many cases it was just painted over. We know children will ingest peeling paint, and if that paint contains lead, the effects on learning downstream are quite severe.

In fact, we could do this nation a great deal of good by offering free inspection of all residences for sources of lead, and low-cost or free methods of remediating it.

Lisa Guernsey suggests we measure access to pre-school and libraries:

Measure whether a community and school district have provided children with access to preschool. Measure how many children have the chance to attend a full-day (versus a half-day) of kindergarten. Measure how much parents are paying for afterschool care and if siblings are being held responsible for that afterschool care instead. Measure whether libraries are partnering with school districts and vice versa. Measure how many parents have easy access to online tools and affordable broadband to be able to follow what is happening in their school districts and enable their children to do their homework.[288]

When I challenged the Gates Foundation to address some of these things directly in the dialogue described in Part III of this book, here was their representative's response:

What we can't do, however, is address all of the problems that put or keep families in poverty. We just don't have the resources to do that. But we are part of a community of donors who are committed to eliminating the causes of poverty.[289]

I will accept that the Gates Foundation may not be able to address all of these problems directly. But according to Bill Gates' 2013 annual letter, the sheer act of measuring things and setting goals around them has tremendous power. I believe his school reform project is failing in large part because it has been measuring the wrong things. If the Gates Foundation is unwilling to tackle the scourge of poverty directly, could it not at least begin to actively measure and set goals for some of the things identified here? Measurement of the things listed – and actions aimed at improving them -- would be far more likely to be successful than the foundation's misguided efforts to increase the capacity of teachers to raise test scores.

Chapter 24

Bill Gates Dances Around the Teacher Evaluation Disaster He Sponsored

No one in America has done more to promote the raising of stakes for test scores in education than Bill Gates.

In April of 2013, Gates published a column that danced around the disaster his advocacy has created in the schools of our nation.[290]

I read his words there, but his actions have spoken so much more loudly, that I could not even make sense out of what he was attempting to say. So allow me to focus first on what Bill Gates has wrought.

No Child Left Behind was headed towards bankruptcy about seven years ago. The practice of labeling schools as failures and closing them, on the basis of test scores, was clearly causing a narrowing of the curriculum. Low income schools in Oakland eliminated art, history and even science in order to focus almost exclusively on math and reading. The arrival of Arne Duncan at the Department of Education (DoEd) and his top level of advisors borrowed from the Gates Foundation created the opportunity for a re-visioning of the project.[291]

Both the *Race to the Top* and the *NCLB* waivers processes required states and districts to put in place teacher and principal evaluation systems which placed "significant" weight on test scores.

The DoEd had told the states how high they had to jump, and the majority did so.

The Gates Foundation promoted these practices not only through their staff members who had migrated to the DoEd , but also through numerous policy and advocacy groups that were well funded, or even created for this purpose. We have the *Data Quality Campaign (DQC)*, the *National Council on Teacher Quality (NCTQ)*, and groups like *Teach Plus*, given millions of dollars to advocate for the use of test scores in teacher evaluations. The *NCTQ*, for example, has asserted that:

> It is fair to say that the school districts in the nation that do the best in the face of the challenge of educating disadvantaged students have become obsessive about using data to drive instruction.[292]

The Gates-funded advocacy group *Teach Plus* organized teachers to testify in favor of a new law in Indiana, which mandated that test scores be used as a significant part of teacher evaluations.[293]

The Gates-funded *Media Bullpen*[294] pushes aggressively for news coverage in education that is critical of unions, and favors the expansion of vouchers and charter schools.[295]

And there are literally hundreds of similar actions that have been taken under the direct sponsorship of the Gates Foundation over the past decade.

That has directly led to the situation that Bill Gates mocked in his April, 2013 column:

> In one Midwestern state,[296] for example, a 166-page Physical Education Evaluation Instrument[297] holds teachers accountable for ensuring that students meet state-defined targets for physical education, such as consistently demonstrating "correct skipping technique with a smooth and effortless rhythm" and "strike consistently a ball with a paddle to a target area with accuracy and good technique." I'm not making this up!

> This is one reason there is a backlash against standardized tests -- in particular, using student test scores as the primary basis for making decisions about firing, promoting and compensating teachers. I'm all for accountability, but I understand teachers' concerns and frustrations.

Where did this PE evaluation come from? It is likely it resulted from language such as that in the Indiana law that Gates proxies got passed in 2011.[298] There, the law passed states:[299]

> A school corporation shall implement the plan beginning with the 2012-2013 school year.
>
> (b) A plan must include the following components:
>
> (1) Performance evaluations for all certificated employees, conducted at least annually.
>
> (2) Objective measures of student achievement and growth to significantly inform the evaluation. The objective measures must include:
>
> (A) student assessment results for certificated employees whose responsibilities include instruction in subjects measured in statewide assessments; and
>
> (B) methods for assessing student growth for certificated employees who do not teach in areas measured by statewide assessments.

That is exactly what the PE teacher evaluation which Bill Gates mocked in his April, 2013 column attempts to do.

This is an echo of a 2013 article co-signed by AFT president Randi Weingarten and Vicki Phillips, which likewise attempted to walk back support for teacher evaluations "done on the quick."[300]

This amounts to an attempt to distance the Gates Foundation from the asinine consequences of the policies they have sponsored, while accepting no responsibility for them whatsoever.

This is a non-starter, as far as I am concerned.

When Bill Gates states he is all for accountability, perhaps he might start with himself. Until then, I really do not value his views on what good accountability systems for others ought to consist of.

Chapter 25

What Will It Take to Educate the Gates Foundation?

Bill Gates and his direct and indirect employees have made a huge gamble.

Let's go back to a 2008 interview with Bill Gates to understand what he hoped would happen:

> There's a lot of issues about governance, whether its school boards or unions, where you want to allow for experimentation, in terms of pay procedures, management procedures, to really prove out new things. As those things start working on behalf of the students, then I believe the majority of teachers and voters will be open-minded to these new approaches. And so we have to take it a step at a time. They have to give us the opportunity for this experimentation.
>
> The cities where our foundation has put the most money in, is where there's a single person responsible - in New York, Chicago, Washington, DC, the mayor has responsibility for the school system, and so instead of having a committee of people, you have that one person. And that's where we've seen the willingness to take on some of the older practices and try new things, and we've seen very good results in all three of those cities, so there are some lessons that have already been learned. We need to make more investments, and I do think the teachers will come along, because after all they're there because they believe in helping the students as well.[301]

Bill Gates has made it clear that this was an experiment from the start. What he did not seem to allow for in his scenario was the possibility that his experiment would not succeed. And there was an impatient imperative in his demands – *"They have to give us the opportunity for this experimentation."*

We, the citizens, students, parents, and educators, were not asked nor allowed to vote on this. Bill Gates and his allies decided this was needed, and they made it happen, using the levers of power within their control.

And this is not an experiment being carried out in a laboratory. It is not even limited to the large cities with mayoral control—because when President Obama was elected, the Gates Foundation had the chance to take its experiment to the national level. Through *Race to the Top* and the subsequent *NCLB*-waiver process, we have had ideas that came from the Gates Foundation turned into federal policies. Here are the big ideas that came from Gates and became federal policy:

- Teacher pay and evaluation systems that must give significant weight to test scores and VAM formulas.

- Unlimited expansion and deregulation of charter schools.

- Creation of Common Core standards and aligned tests and curriculum.

These strategies were driven by three big assumptions. The first was that data—mainly in the form of test scores—would provide ever more timely and specific information that could be used not only to "personalize" instruction, but also to scientifically measure learning. When this data was connected to evaluation and compensation systems in schools, this would drive continuous improvement, and weed out those teachers who were not effective.

The second major assumption was that market competition would drive improvement, both in schools themselves, and in the ever-more-important field of educational technology. This is a bit complex. In terms of schools, the Gates Foundation pushed - and the Department of Education adopted - policies that removed limits from the expansion of

charter schools.[302] This has led to a significant expansion in these schools across the country, the idea being that removing charter schools from the fetters of school district management and union representation would yield innovation, and that forcing schools to compete for students would lead to improvement.

The third assumption was that educators had used poverty to excuse their own failings, and that high expectations for schools, teachers, and students would lead to greatly improved outcomes. And these high expectations needed to be enforced through real consequences for failure at every level. "Our students cannot wait" for poverty to be addressed, goes the argument, and education itself is the way out of poverty. If we fire our worst teachers, Gates asserted on Oprah in 2010, our standing on international test rankings would soar to the top.[303]

In our dialogue (see chapters 10 to 14) I attempted to point out to the Gates Foundation the flaws in these assumptions and the strategies they yielded. Even then, there were already solid reasons to doubt the wisdom of these reforms.

Gates proved right in one regard, in that we "had to" give this approach a chance. We had no choice, because Gates and his allies in government and industry made the decisions for us. But today, the experiment has yielded plenty of data that allows us to reach some rather disturbing conclusions.

A report released in April, 2013, by the nonprofit advocacy group *Broader, Bolder Approach to Education* took a close look at the big cities—the very ones cited by Bill Gates in his 2008 remarks (quoted above) as being models of reform, and found that rather than being showcases of success, they have yielded poor results overall.[304]

The report finds that the reforms deliver few benefits, often harm the students they purport to help, and divert attention from a set of other, less visible policies with more promise to weaken the link between poverty and low educational attainment.

In April, 2104, the *American Statistical Association* issued a definitive report condemning the use of VAM systems to evaluate teachers. The report states:

Most VAM studies find that teachers account for about 1% to 14% of the variability in test scores, and that the majority of opportunities for quality improvement are found in the system-level conditions. Ranking teachers by their VAM scores can have unintended consequences that reduce quality.[305]

This reinforces a 2011 joint statement by the *American Educational Research Association* and the *National Academy of Education:*

> With respect to value-added measures of student achievement tied to individual teachers, current research suggests that high-stakes, individual-level decisions, or comparisons across highly dissimilar schools or student populations, should be avoided.[306]

Meanwhile these systems are yielding the haphazard results that experts have warned against from the start—teachers of the year fired for inadequate scores,[307] and those who teach English Learners or special education students unfairly labeled ineffective.

Research on charter schools continues to provide evidence that they rarely outperform public schools, and often divert essential support from them. Virtual charters tend to be worst of all, yet continue to receive public funds.[308] Even in Chicago, where Arne Duncan and Rahm Emanuel have provided extensive support, charters have failed to show themselves any better than regular public schools.[309]

Charters have been part of a pattern of increased segregation,[310] and have been found to leave some of the neediest students behind.[311] Policymakers in both Chile[312] and Sweden[313] are now attempting to undo the tremendous damage the diversion of public funds to private schools has done to their public schools.

While a few charters, like one I visited in Albuquerque in 2012,[314] have been truly innovative, the sector as a whole has been a bust, especially if the intention was to show that poverty should not matter to school success.

The grand alignment that was to be achieved through the Common Core is likewise faltering. As Diane Ravitch pointed out in March, 2014, the standard-setting process failed to follow established processes that make such standards legitimate.[315] As the tests arrive and declare our students and schools to be worse than ever, their validity faces even more questions. A growing opt-out movement threatens to bring the entire data-driven enterprise to its knees, and parental concerns about student privacy have already led to the demise of the Gates-funded inBloom data storage system.[316]

In April, 2014, a study was released by Princeton University's Martin Gilens and Benjamin I. Page, which suggests that:

> ...economic elites and organized groups representing business interests have substantial independent impacts on U.S. government policy, while average citizens and mass-based interest groups have little or no independent influence.[317]

Clearly, teacher unions are a "mass-based interest group", but teachers and their unions do not have any significant power in our schools, or in policies affecting education. Instead, it is organizations like the Gates, Broad and Walton foundations, and business alliances like *ALEC* that are running the reform show. Last September, Bill Gates said, "It would be great if our education stuff worked, but that we won't know for probably a decade."[318]

I think we already know enough to declare the experiment a failure.

- VAM is a disaster. Any "reformer" who continues to support giving significant weight to such unreliable indicators should lose any credibility.

- Charter schools are, as a sector, not better than public schools, are expanding segregation, and increasing inequality.

- The Common Core and the high stakes accountability system in which it is embedded is on its way to the graveyard of grand ideas.

The only question remaining is how long Gates and his employees and proxies will remain wedded to their ideas and continue to push them through their sponsored advocacy, even when these policies have been proven to be ill-founded and unworkable.

Part of the problem with market-driven reform is that when you introduce the opportunity to make money off something like education, you unleash a feedback loop. Companies like the virtual charter chain *K12 Inc* can make tremendous profits, which they can then use to buy off politicians, given our Supreme Court's "Corporations are people and money is speech" philosophy. There are no systemic brakes on this train. The only way turn this around is for people to organize in large enough numbers, and act together in ways that actively disrupt and derail the operation.

Chapter 26

Accountability for Gates: The Billionaire Philanthropist Evaluation

Bill Gates, who is more responsible than anyone for the absurd evaluations by which teachers are now being held accountable, had the gall to write in 2013 in a tone of exasperation about the results of his own advocacy for these very practices (see Chapter 24).

I have long wondered when the great enthusiast for accountability for others might hold himself accountable for his own handiwork.

As wealth has concentrated in the accounts of individuals such as the Gates, Walton and Broad families, they have used this to wield unprecedented power over the lives of those of us without access to such resources. They pay for research that creates the supposed "facts" which they then use to frame the public debate. They pay for their own media outlets, and heavily subsidize others. Their money redirects existing grassroots groups, and underwrites new ones. They work with *ALEC* to write legislation, and funnel money through PACs to buy off politicians to move this legislation forward across the country. They are utterly insulated from any sort of accountability. They do not face voters in any election. Nobody "evaluates" them. They cannot be fired. They may on occasion choose to engage in dialogue, but they are not obliged to respond to the substance of the criticisms raised. As my question indicated, this accountability they demand from teachers is a street that goes one way only.

But let's imagine we could turn the tables on Bill Gates and evaluate his performance as a philanthropist. Might we establish some goals to which we could hold our billionaires accountable? We do not have any measurable indicators such as test scores to use, but since I do not find these to be of great value in any case, I will offer a more qualitative metric, based on my knowledge of the Gates' philanthropic work. Since he has spoken glowingly of the salutary effect of feedback on teachers, surely he will welcome this feedback, even though it is unsolicited.

In the tradition of the Danielson[319] and Marzano[320] teacher evaluation frameworks, I offer the *Cody Billionaire Philanthropist Evaluation Model*, as applied to Bill Gates.

Standard 1: Awareness of the Social Conditions Targeted by Philanthropy

Rating: *Below Standard*

Bill Gates does not demonstrate an understanding of the social conditions that are the focus of his philanthropy. Actions and statements by him and his representatives indicate ignorance of the pervasive effects of poverty, and the overwhelming research that indicates the need to address these effects directly. Bill Gates has not worked in an educational context, and thus he has no personal expertise. He primarily cites research he has paid for himself, which tends to conform to his views. His representatives have claimed that his foundation lacks the resources to address poverty directly, and insists that educators bear the burden for overcoming its effects with minimal support.

Recommendation for Professional Growth:

We recommend Bill Gates take a year off from his work as a philanthropist, and work as a high school instructor in an urban setting. His students should include English learners, students who are homeless, and those designated as Special Education. He should work alongside a fully credentialed professional educator, who will provide him with feedback, and reflect with him as he gains an understanding of how to create effective learning conditions for such students.

Standard 2: Understanding of how Learning is Measured

Rating: *Below Standard*

Bill Gates has concluded that measurement is the primary means by which social progress can be made. He has determined that test scores are an adequate means of measuring learning, and has promoted a wide variety of ways by which these scores are used to measure learning, and reward teachers and students accordingly. This is based on a fundamental error. In fact, test scores measure only a small part of what we value.

Recommendations for Professional Growth:

Bill Gates should first read Stephen Jay Gould's *Mismeasure of Man*[321] for an understanding of the history of testing. He should also read Daniel Koretz' book, *Measuring Up, What Educational Testing Really Tells Us*.[322]

Bill Gates should, with the help of an experienced educator, design a series of rich projects that allows each of his students to demonstrate their learning through authentic products in real-world contexts. He should compare the work they are capable of producing to their standardized test scores, and reflect on the things that each mode of measurement captures.

Standard 3: Understanding of How Teaching is Evaluated

Rating: *Below Standard*

Compounding the fundamental error regarding the measurement of learning described under Standard 2 above, Bill Gates has promoted the use of teacher evaluations based in significant part on student test scores and VAM systems. Research does not support such use of test scores, and raising the stakes on test scores has promoted widespread practices of "teaching to the test". Bill Gates has made statements that indicate he is unaware of effective evaluation practices, such as the *Peer Assistance and Review (PAR)* program[323] and others.

Recommendations for Professional Growth:

Bill Gates should spend a week shadowing PAR consulting teachers as they work with teachers in Toledo, Ohio. He should review the research on various forms of effective evaluation practices.

As recommended above, he should serve as a classroom teacher for a full year, and have his performance rated based on VAM scores derived from standardized tests taken by his students. He should reflect with his colleagues on the validity of these ratings. He should also meet with a peer evaluator to set professional goals for himself at the start of the year, and several times during the year meet with this person to reflect on his progress. At year's end he should compare the models of evaluation he experienced, and reflect on which were of greater validity and value.

Standard 4: Understanding of Effective Instruction

Rating: *Below Standard*

Bill Gates has repeatedly stated that he believes we ought to stop spending money on keeping class sizes small, and instead should use that money to provide performance bonuses for teachers. He has also indicated that we should "personalize" learning through the use of computers and videos that allow students to work at their own pace. This does not comport with what we know about child development, or the importance of personal relationships with students.

Recommendations for Professional Growth:

Bill Gates should spend a week shadowing children in elite schools such as the one attended by his own children, and study the way personalization is accomplished. He should then spend a week shadowing children at a Detroit school where class sizes have been significantly increased due to budget cuts, and where the pressures of high stakes testing have focused instruction on test preparation.

In the year he teaches, he should be assigned at least one class no larger than 15, and another no smaller than 38, and reflect on the learning conditions in these two environments.

Summary of Evaluation Results and Recommendations:

Bill Gates falls below standards in all four of the areas that were observed. His philanthropic activities should be suspended immediately pending his completion of the recommended professional growth activities.

A panel of expert reviewers composed of students, parents and educators from communities that are the targets of his philanthropy should be convened to review his reflections at the end of his year of investigation and reflection. This panel should subsequently review and approve the re-initiation of his philanthropic projects following this evaluation process.

This is the beginning of what might be a far more complex process of reflection for Bill Gates. It might be seen as absurd, but my intention is sincere. His thinking is magnified in its effect by the billions he has to spend as he chooses. With such power comes a huge responsibility to learn from one's mistakes. I do not know how Bill Gates reflects on the successes and failures of his work - there is no evidence of any significant thoughtful reflection in his public writing.

Fairness demands that accountability cannot be a one way street. If Bill Gates demands that teachers be held accountable for their work, surely he must accept some accountability for his. What is good for the poor geese ought to be good for the billionaire gander, even if he does lay golden eggs.

Chapter 27

On Motives and Markets: Breaking the Big Taboo

When Lyndsey Layton interviewed Bill Gates in 2014, she violated one of the major taboos of the education reform discourse. She suggested that he needed to respond to concerns being raised about his personal financial motives in supporting the Common Core.

Here is her question, as transcribed by Mercedes Schneider:[324]

Layton: There are some people who, when they hear the speech that you just gave where you were talking about standardization and common standards will help drive innovation and help us have this, the online revolution in a way that, that this part of the economy has really been untouched; that it's important that if we have common standards, then we can really open up the online, the benefits of the online revolution in education. There are people who hear that and think, 'That's what he's doing. He really wants this because he wants to encourage the technology industry because he's the cofounder of Microsoft. It's, it's, he's being driven by business interests here.' What, how would you respond to that?

Gates' response is interesting. At first he pretends to not even understand what Layton could possibly be suggesting:

Gates: Uh, I think, you're, you're sticking to the political side of this thing. Uhh...

Layton: I'm from the *Washington Post*. We're in Washington.

Gates: Do you think that passes, do you think that passes muster?

Layton: I, I don't *know*. I am not, I, this is the first time we've met...

Gates: Okay, so give me the, give me the logic here.

Layton: The logic is...

Gates: What is it that you're saying? It's all a lot of self-interest? It's...

Layton: That, no, that that's, that that's one of the driving forces behind your embrace of the Common Core.

Gates: Meaning what?

Layton: Meaning Microsoft and Pearson just signed a deal to, to put the Common Core curriculum on the surface. So, you've got a product, Microsoft has a product now that it's, that it's selling...

Gates: Yeah, we had the old Pearson stuff. I, it, it, there's no connection, there's no connection to Common Core and any Microsoft thing.

Layton: Okay. Well I just, I want to understand this, but that's a, Bill, let me just tell you...

Gates: That's staying away from the substance, okay?

Layton: But it's a question when people know, when people learn that you are promoting the Common Core...

Gates: Do you seriously think that the reason I like the Common Core is for some self-interested reason? That's what you're saying.

Layton: No, no. *I don't* know that I believe that, and you don't seem...

Gates: You don't know. You *don't know?*

Layton: I don't think that I believe that.

[Gates rolls his eyes and smiles.]

Layton: Okay, that's kind of a pertinent question that a lot of people who, uh, who *don't* know you, are (asking), are wondering, and I would just like some response to. But, you're saying you don't want to talk about that, or you don't want to...

Gates: I'm saying, and I've, I hope I can make this clear, I believe in the Common Core because of its substance and what it will do to improve education, and that's the *only* reason I believe in the Common Core. And I have *no*, you know, this is *giving money* away. This is philanthropy. This is trying to make sure students have the kind of opportunity *I* had. You, You've, there is *nothing*, uh, it's so, almost... outrageous to say otherwise in my view.

This exchange is worth examining. In order to get Gates to even answer the question, the journalist must first stipulate that while she personally does not believe the accusation, she still would like Gates to respond to those who may.

And actually, in listening to the video myself I heard something not in Schneider's original transcript. At the most tense part of the exchange, at minute 16:30, just before Layton says "I don't think that I believe that," a male voice from off camera says "why don't we move on?"

The question is clearly an affront to Gates. It is "almost outrageous" to suggest that anything but altruism is behind Gates' passionate advocacy and financial sponsorship of the Common Core.

This was quite possibly the first time a reporter had the nerve to ask Gates such a direct question regarding Common Core. Those of us who have raised questions regarding the motives of various sponsors of education reform are accustomed to being accused of being "conspiracy theorists." This is a marker for statements or inquiries that violate the norms of discourse. This is a form of social taboo, and marginalizes the "conspiracy theorist" as a kook.

I have actually never accused Gates of pursuing education reform for the sake of personal financial gain. I have no way of knowing if this is the case. It is true that, as Valerie Strauss pointed out recently, Gates may indeed profit from Common Core as a result of Microsoft's various projects related to the new standards.[325]

But given that Gates is the richest man in the world, he may not want even more wealth - I really don't know. Do the rich ever seem to say "that's enough" wealth and power? Maybe they do!

Here is the deeper problem with Gates' model for education reform. It is built on a vision for social change that asserts that in order for the needs of the poor to be met effectively, the drive for profit must be unleashed. Gates views this as the driving force for innovation.

In 2007, Gates returned to Harvard, which he had attended but not graduated from, to give a commencement speech. Here is part of what he said:

> We can make market forces work better for the poor if we can develop a more creative capitalism - if we can stretch the reach of market forces so that more people can make a profit, or at least make a living, serving people who are suffering from the worst inequities. We also can press governments around the world to spend taxpayer money in ways that better reflect the values of the people who pay the taxes.

> If we can find approaches that meet the needs of the poor in ways that generate profits for business and votes for politicians, we will have found a sustainable way to reduce inequity in the world.[326]

In Gates' view, the way to meet the needs of the poor is to make it profitable for corporations to do so. The simple fact that a drive for profits is far more often the source of poverty than a solution to it has escaped him.

This model does not allow for a robust and independent public sector that is under the democratic control of citizens. Instead, the public system must be re-engineered so that the funds continue to flow from taxpayers, but flow into various profit-seeking enterprises competing against one another. The only thing that stays "public" is the source of the funding.

It is largely irrelevant whether Gates himself is motivated by a desire to increase his vast wealth. His model for education reform is powered by the drive for profits, and his "reforms" all seem to unleash this drive in one way or another. His "philanthropy" is aimed at pushing the institution of education from the public sphere into the realm of the private, the corporate. Here are the strategies that go into this:

- Measure student outcomes by test scores so that schools, teachers, students, and various competing "learning systems" can be judged, and marked as successes or failures.[327]

- Promote mayoral control and undermine locally elected school boards, so as to allow for maximum leeway for reform "experiments."[328]

- Create a system of national tests so "innovations" can be compared and marketed on a national scale.[329]

- Promote semi-private charter schools, with little public oversight or union representation.[330]

- Undermine traditional schools of education, and promote "alternative" means of preparing teachers. Push for the evaluation of such programs to be based on the test scores of the students of their teacher graduates.[331]

All of these "reforms" undermine the democratic control of our public education system, and wherever possible, shift control into testing companies, private ventures, or individuals subject to corporate influence.

Every week we read of some new scandal associated with charter schools. A recent investigation by *Integrity in Education* focused on only 15 states found more than $100 million has been diverted into private pockets.[332] Software and testing systems routinely deliver flawed data, with very little accountability.[333] We get a regular charade of supposed champions of civil rights insisting that we must have high quality teachers while at the same time awarding grants to *Teach For America*, promoting the use of teachers with only five weeks of training in the nation's most challenging schools.[334]

Market-based solutions have a major flaw. When profit is used as the motivator, the most needy students are not served well. The measurement systems that the Gates Foundation has promoted, such as

VAM based teacher evaluations, actually punish teachers who work with the neediest students.[335] Charter schools have been found to consistently under-enroll the neediest special ed students, leaving that burden to the public schools.[336] Charter schools are increasing the level of segregation in many cities.[337] Solutions based on technological innovations, so beloved by Gates, have yet to reduce inequities - and may even increase them, as recent research suggests.[338]

However, so long as profits are being made, the inadequacies of these "solutions" can be masked, because the corporations making money can provide active financial support to lawmakers willing to give them support, and few in the media are willing to run the risk of incurring the epithets of the billionaires they might offend by uncovering the unsavory side of reform.

I am glad Layton asked Gates that question about his personal financial motives, even if we never do get a clear answer. What is clear is that his model for education reform places the motive for profits in the driver's seat, and our recent experiences with profit seeking corporations suggests that this will make for a very rough ride for the rest of us.

The failure of market-driven solutions to educational problems offers us a chance to try something different. It is time to re-invest in the democratic processes in our cities. It is time to tap the energy of innovation within our schools, by freeing them from intense pressure to increase test scores. We need to put the ***public*** back into public education, and for once, provide adequate resources to our schools, especially those with the neediest students.

Epilogue

In Order to Motivate Our Students We Must Change Their Futures From Bleak to Bright

As we conclude, I am trying to make sense of corporate education reform, which seems a mass of contradictions. On the one hand, we have a seemingly utopian project with bold pronouncements about the boundless capacity of all students - even those with serious learning disabilities - to succeed on ever more difficult tests. On the other hand, we have Common Core-aligned tests that are apparently intentionally designed to fail two thirds of our students.[339] In order to break through the confusion, I have focused on the thinking of one of the chief architects and financial sponsors of corporate reform, Bill Gates.

In a June, 2014 visit to Los Alamos, Gates responded to questions about the success of educational technologies this way:

New technology to engage students holds some promise, but Gates says it tends to only benefit those who are motivated.

"And the one thing we have a lot of in the United States is unmotivated students," Gates said. [340]

It is a bit ironic that Gates offers the "excuse" of poor student motivation for the failure of technology, when the "no excuses" reform movement he has sponsored allows for no such excuses for teachers and schools. Nonetheless, the connection between student success and their internal motivation is a huge and important insight, because it is the clue that tells us there are limits to the degree to which we can manipulate others. Human agency is ultimately a determining factor. And once we begin to explore the motivation of our students - or lack thereof, we can

172

learn some very important things.

I think one of the key pieces that Gates has missed with his approach to education is the connection between students' motivation and their life prospects. This goes beyond the material conditions of poverty that directly impinge on students' capacity to learn - neighborhood violence, hunger, unstable housing and so on. This has to do with what students perceive are their opportunities in life. These perceptions are influenced by what students see around them. How are older relatives and friends in the neighborhood doing after graduating from high school? Is the promised path of high school diploma, followed by four-year degree, actually working out? Or are they seeing older peers forced to drop out, or graduating saddled with debt,[341] without the high-paying jobs that might justify such an investment?

In an interview at the American Enterprise Institute, Gates himself recently observed that future job prospects are likely to be significantly diminished in the decades to come as a result of technological advances. Gates says:

> Well, technology in general will make capital more attractive than labor over time. Software substitution, you know, whether it's for drivers or waiters or nurses... It's progressing. And that's going to force us to rethink how these tax structures work in order to maximize employment, you know, given that, you know, capitalism in general, over time, will create more inequality and technology, over time, will reduce demand for jobs particularly at the lower end of the skill set. And so, you know, we have to adjust, and these things are coming fast. Twenty years from now, labor demand for lots of skill sets will be substantially lower, and I don't think people have that in their mental model.[342]

What Gates calls "software substitution" is the replacement of human workers with robots, driverless cars, or other technologically based innovations. But he might be surprised to find out how many people already living in poverty and the dwindling middle class have adjusted their mental models to this reality of 21st century America. And if people do not see opportunities available to them as a result of their education, they are likely to disengage.

In a 2014 interview with Jeremy Paxman, Gates makes clear that the *gap* between rich and poor is of little concern. Instead, he focuses on poverty - but take a look at how poverty and the middle class are defined:

> **Paxman**: When you hear that statistic from Oxfam that the poorest half of the world own about as much as the 85 richest, including you of course, does that make you feel uncomfortable?
>
> **Gates**: Well we... What makes me uncomfortable is that children die, that people don't get a good education, they don't get enough nutrition and that's what I've devoted my life working on. So all the money in my hands is going against those problems.
>
> **Paxman**: But you don't deny that the gap between rich and poor seems to have got worse?
>
> **Gates**: The gap between rich and poor has *not* gotten worse, thank goodness. Less children are dying, people are living longer, people are more literate. If you go back far enough, everybody was poor. If you want everybody to be the same like 200 years ago when life was very short, a third of all children died before they were five years old. That was an age of strong equality.[343]

In this interview with Rolling Stone, Gates' view of poverty becomes clearer. Gates says:

> Poverty today looks very different than poverty in the past. The real thing you want to look at is consumption and use that as a metric and say, "Have you been worried about having enough to eat? Do you have enough warmth, shelter? Do you think of yourself as having a place to go?" The poor are better off than they were before, even though they're still in the bottom group in terms of income.[344]

Gates' interview at the American Enterprise Institute reveals a bit more about how he believes we might address the problem of poverty:

> Well, I think economists would have said that a progressive consumption tax is a better construct, you know, at any point in history. The idea that through the income tax credit you would end up with a certain minimum wage that you'd receive, that I understand better than potentially damping demand in the part of the labor

spectrum that I'm most worried about.[345]

To put this more clearly, Gates is suggesting we increase taxes on consumption by the wealthy, and use those revenues to provide a sort of subsistence level payment to the poor. He opposes an increase in the minimum wage because it might raise employer costs, which they would then try to cut by laying people off.

Gates is unconcerned about income inequality as an issue. He defines poverty as abject starvation and homelessness, and hopes employers can be convinced to keep employees because they do not cost very much.

The motivation of 50 million K12 students in the US is directly related to the degree to which their education leads to a brighter future. We have a big disconnect here when the future does not, in fact, offer much chance at access to college or productive employment. And as Wilkinson and Pickett established in their book *The Spirit Level*, the level of inequality a society tolerates has a dramatic effect on the mental state and wellbeing of its citizens.[346]

How does this connect to Gates' Common Core project? There is solid evidence that the 30% pass rate on Common Core-aligned tests in New York was not an accident, but was planned by testing officials.[347] Those in charge of the tests are making an intentional decision regarding how many students pass or fail. A 30% pass rate on Common Core tests is not some objective statement regarding how many students are ready for career and college. It is a predetermined outcome, which has a whole set of assumptions in it regarding what "college and career ready" means. Mark Weber (Jersey Jazzman) explains exactly what those assumptions are based on - things like the loose correlations between test scores and college freshmen GPA and SAT scores.[348]

Note that the end result is that 70% of the students taking the Common Core tests are rated as failures, not "ready for college and career." And for English Learners and African American students the failure rates are much higher.

Carol Burris and John Murphy have analyzed the tests that New York plans to use to decide who will receive a high school diploma, and discovered that only about 25% of the students will pass.[349]

Now we come to a very strange and disturbing coincidence.

Recent changes in the GED are having some drastic effects on students. The GED is used in lieu of a high school diploma, as a gateway to a college education. The new GED test has been taken over by Pearson, and is now aligned to the Common Core.[350] The result is a test that is so difficult that there has been an 80% drop in the number of students passing it.

If we accept that the low pass rates we are seeing on Common Core-aligned tests are not an accident, but are the result of their design, this indicates there is an attempt to use ever more difficult Common Core aligned tests to certify as many as two thirds of our students as unworthy of the opportunity to have a career or attend college.

This raises the possibility of a dystopian future where an underclass of Common Core test rejects is allowed to subsist with the bare minimum payments required to keep starvation at bay, while a shrinking cadre of insecure workers maintain the machinery that keep the lights on and the crops harvested.

The fundamental problem of the current economy is that we have not figured out a means by which the top 1% can be persuaded to share the prodigious profits that have flowed to them from technological advances.

In some regards Gates' understanding and mine are not that far apart.

While in his response to Paxman he bristles at the idea that the gap between rich and poor has widened, as noted earlier, in the more relaxed setting of his interview at the American Enterprise Institute, he states:

...given that, you know, capitalism in general, over time, will create more inequality and technology, over time, will reduce demand for jobs particularly at the lower end of the skill set...

So we agree there. But I cannot reconcile how this future of growing inequality and a shrinking workforce intersects with the grand utopian vision of the Common Core of preparing all students for career and college. So then I go back and have to question the validity of the promises made for the Common Core, since the economic projection Gates is making here seems sound.

While Gates is advocating some sort of adjustments to tax policy to transfer a bit of wealth downward, I do not see any serious efforts on his part in this arena. Our elite, including Gates, do not seem terribly interested in any sort of restructuring of the economic relationships that have them accruing tremendous wealth and power.

These economic problems will not be addressed by Common Core, by charter schools or any other educational reforms. They will not even be addressed in a significant way by what we might praise as authentic education reforms, such as smaller class sizes or more time for teacher collaboration - though these are worthwhile and humane things.

Imperfect as they have been, public schools have been an institution under mostly democratic control, funded by taxpayers, governed by elected school boards, and run by career educators. Market-driven education reform is bringing the cruelty of commerce into what was part of the public sphere, attempting to use test scores to open and close schools like shoe stores, and paying teachers on test score commissions as if we were salesmen.

The rhetoric of the corporate reform project draws on the modern movement for civil rights, and even Bill Gates asserts that his goal is to fight inequity. But elites have rarely, if ever, designed solutions that diminish their privilege, and corporate education reform is no exception. It appears that such reformers have devised a means to affix the blame for inequity on classroom teachers, even as technological advances make it possible to transfer even more wealth into reform sponsors' bank accounts, with fewer people being paid for the work that remains necessary. The promise that the Common Core will prepare everyone for the American dream is made a lie by the intentionally engineered failure rates on Common Core aligned tests.

The fundamental problem educators face is that it is very difficult to inspire and motivate students whose future is bleak. And the ever more difficult Common Core tests actually make this task even more difficult - as they certify a major portion of our population as unworthy of career or college. This will also reinforce established patterns of racial inequity.

As educators understand this disconnect, there will be greater resistance to this bait and switch. And this resistance will find allies among our students, the debt-burdened college graduates, those in communities abandoned by the modern economy, the many millions rendered surplus by an economy that does not need them, and those still clinging to their piece of the dream. The sooner this set of illusions is exploded, the sooner we can begin the real challenge of reshaping our economic system so that it gives our students the opportunities they deserve.

References

1. Cody, Anthony (Jan. 30, 2011). TeamScience Tames Teacher Turnover in Oakland, *Education Week/Teacher*, Retrieved from http://blogs.edweek.org/teachers/livin-in-dialogue/2011/01/teamscience_tames_teacher_turn.html

2. *Waiting for Superman* (2010). Excerpt. [Video file]. Retrieved from http://movieclips.com/xhyus-waiting-for-superman-movie-bill-gates/

3. Foundation Fact Sheet, Bill & Melinda Gates Foundation. Retrieved July 25, 2014, from http://www.gatesfoundation.org/Who-We-Are/General-Information/Foundation-Factsheet

4. Dillon, Sam. (May 21, 2011). Behind Grass-Roots School Advocacy, Bill Gates, *New York Times*. Retrieved from http://www.nytimes.com/2011/05/22/education/22gates.html

5. Bill and Melinda Gates Foundation. How We Work. Retrieved July 25, 2014 from: http://www.gatesfoundation.org/How-We-Work/Quick-Links/Grants-Database/Grants/2011/11/OPP1049802

6. Holtzman, Clay. (May 17, 2009). Growing DC presence for Gates Foundation, *Puget Sound Business Journal*. Retrieved from: http://www.bizjournals.com/seattle/stories/2009/05/18/story2.html

7. McNeil, Michele. (Sep. 23, 2009). UPDATED: Gates Spreading 'Race to the Top' Help to All States. *Education Week*. Retrieved from http://blogs.edweek.org/edweek/campaign-k-12/2009/09/all_states_now_eligible_for_ga.html

8. Layton, Lyndsey (June 7, 2014). How Bill Gates Pulled off the Swift Common Core Revolution. *Washington Post*, Retrieved from: http://www.washingtonpost.com/politics/how-bill-gates-pulled-off-the-swift-common-core-revolution/2014/06/07/a830e32e-ec34-11e3-9f5c-9075d5508f0a_story.html

9. Schneider, Mercedes (Feb. 24, 2014). The Gates Grant Addiction. *Deutsch29 Blog*. Retrieved from: http://deutsch29.wordpress.com/2014/02/24/the-gates-grant-addiction

10. Gilens, Martin & Page, Benjamin (Apr. 9, 2014). The Transformation of American Politics: Activist Government and the Rise of Conservatism. Retrieved from: http://www.princeton.edu/%7Emgilens/Gilens%20homepage%20materials/Gilens%20and%20Page/Gilens%20and%20Page%202014-Testing%20Theories%203-7-14.pdf

11. Shaw, Linda (June 8, 2013). Gates Foundation Looking to Make Nice with Teachers." *Seattle Times*. Retrieved from: http://seattletimes.com/html/education/2021149398_gatesfoundationteachersxml.html

12. Dillon, Sam (Apr. 27, 2011). "Foundations Join to Offer Online Courses for Schools." *The New York Times*. Retrieved from http://www.nytimes.com/2011/04/28/education/28gates.html

13. Libby, Ken (Aug. 11, 2010). What Shelton's Waiver Tells Us About the Gates Foundation and DOE. *Schools Matter*. Retrieved from: http://www.schoolsmatter.info/2010/07/what-shelton-waiver-tells-us-about.html

14. Gates, Bill, and Melinda (Oct. 22, 2011). Grading the Teachers. *The Wall Street Journal*. Retrieved from: http://online.wsj.com/article/SB1000142405297020448530457664112376700651 8.html

15. National Board for Professional Teaching Standards (NBPTS). *The Five Core Propositions*. Retrieved July 25, 2014, from http://nbpts.org/five-core-propositions

16. Sawchuk, Stephen (Mar. 5 2011). National Board Urged to Consider Student Test Scores. *Education Week*. Retrieved from: http://www.edweek.org/ew/articles/2011/03/16/26nbpts.h30.html

17. Shah, Nirvi (Nov. 4, 2011). Academic Gains Vary Widely for Charter Networks. *Education Week*. Retrieved from: http://www.edweek.org/ew/articles/2011/11/04/11charter.h31.html

18. Measures of Effective Teaching Project. Retrieved July 25, 2014, from http://www.metproject.org/

19. Bill & Melinda Gates Foundation: Teach Plus, Incorporated (Sept. 2009). Retrieved from: http://www.gatesfoundation.org/How-We-Work/Quick-Links/Grants-Database/Grants/2009/09/OPP1003735

20. Birch, B. A. (Oct. 14, 2011). Education Nation Sponsors' Roles Face Scrutiny. *Education News*. Retrieved from: http://www.educationnews.org/education-policy-and-politics/education-nation-sponsors%E2%80%99-roles-face-scrutiny/

21. Waiting for Superman (2010).

22. Cody, Anthony (Sep. 23, 2010). How WOULD a Journalist Cover Education Nation? *Education Week/Teacher*. Retrieved from http://blogs.edweek.org/teachers/living-in-dialogue/2010/09/how_would_a_journalist_cover_e.html

23. Education Nation Teacher Town Hall (Sep. 25, 2011). Transcript of broadcast by Anthony Cody.

24. Hunter, John (Mar. 2011). Teaching with the World Peace Game. *TED.com*, Retrieved from https://www.ted.com/talks/john_hunter_on_the_world_peace_game

25. Roberts, Georgett (Feb. 26, 2012). Queens Parents Demand Answers following Teacher's Low Grades. *New York Post*. Retrieved from: http://www.nypost.com/p/news/local/cursed_with_the_worst_in_queens_f5wLhEdDRN1Wl9h1GQgxAM

26. Gates, Bill (Feb. 22, 2012). Shame Is Not the Solution. *The New York Times*. Retrieved from: http://www.nytimes.com/2012/02/23/opinion/for-teachers-shame-is-no-solution.html

27. The Shocking State of Our Schools (Sept. 20, 2010). *Oprah.com*. Retrieved from: http://www.oprah.com/oprahshow/The-Shocking-State-of-Our-Schools

28. Toppo, Greg (Feb. 16, 2012) U.S. Schools' International Rank Gets Boost. *USA Today*. Retrieved from: http://www.usatoday.com/USCP/PNI/Nation/World/2012-02-16-bcUSATSCHOOLSRANKINGSCX_ST_U.htm

29. Measures of Effective Teaching. *MET Project*. Retrieved July 25, 2014, from http://www.metproject.org/

30. Lucido, Rog (Feb 27, 2012). Student Learning Can Only Be Described, Not Measured, *Education Week/Teacher*, Retrieved from http://blogs.edweek.org/teachers/living-in-dialogue/2012/02/rog_lucido_we_cannot_measure_s.html

31. Accomplished California Teachers (2010). A Quality Teacher in Every Classroom: An Evaluation System that Works for California. Retrieved from: http://nbrc.stanford.edu/act/reports/a-quality-teacher-in-every-classroom.html

32. Rubinstein, Gary (Feb. 28, 2012). Analyzing NYC Value-Added Data, Part 2, *Gary Rubinstein's Blog*. Retrieved from: http://garyrubinstein.teachforus.org/2012/02/28/analyzing-released-nyc-value-added-data-part-2/

33. MET Project (2010). Learning about Teaching: Initial Findings from the Measures of Effective Teaching Project. Retrieved from: http://www.metproject.org/downloads/Preliminary_Finding-Policy_Brief.pdf

34. Merrow, John (Apr. 4, 2012). A Trifecta Of Sins, *Taking Note blog*. Retrieved from: http://takingnote.learningmatters.tv/?p=5681

35. Henion, Geary (Apr. 13, 2012). Charter Schools Spend More on Administration than Public Schools. Retrieved from: http://msutoday.msu.edu/news/2012/charter-schools-spend-more-on-administration-than-public-schools/

36. CREDO (2009). Multiple Choice: Charter School Performance in 16 States, Retrieved from: http://credo.stanford.edu/reports/MULTIPLE_CHOICE_EXECUTIVE SUMMARY.pdf

37. Song, Jason and Felch, Jason (May 7, 2011). Times updates and expands value-added ratings for Los Angeles elementary school teachers. *Los Angeles Times*. Retrieved from http://www.latimes.com/local/la-me-value-added-20110508-story.html#page=1

38. Roberts, Georgett (Feb. 26, 2012). Queens parents demand answers following teacher's low grades, *New York Post*. Retrieved from http://nypost.com/2012/02/26/queens-parents-demand-answers-following-teachers-low-grades/

39. Clowes, George (Nov. 1, 1999). Helping Teachers Raise Student Achievement: An Interview with William L. Sanders. *Heartlander Magazine*. Retrieved from: http://news.heartland.org/newspaper-article/1999/11/01/helping-teachers-raise-student-achievement-interview-william-l-sanders

40. Weiss, Joanne (Mar. 31, 2011). The Innovation Mismatch: 'Smart Capital' and Education Innovation, *Harvard Business Review blog*. Retrieved from: http://blogs.hbr.org/innovations-in-education/2011/03/the-innovation-mismatch-smart.html

41. Professional Development & Instruction. A-List, Retrieved July 25, 2014, from http://alisteducation.com/afterschool-programs

42. AP, Honors & Electives. *Pearson Corporation*. Retrieved July 25, 2014, from http://pearsonschool.com/index.cfm?locator=PSZu6s&acornRdt=1&DCSext.w_psvaniturl=http%3A%2F%2Fwww%2Epearsonschool%2Ecom%2Fadvanced

43. Cramer, Philissa (Apr. 12, 2012). Investigation into charter CEO ends with an indictment, *Chalkbeat*. Retrieved from http://gothamschools.org/2012/04/12/investigation-into-charter-school-ceo-ends-with-an-indictment/

44. ASCD. Retrieved July 25, 2014, from http://www.ascd.org

45. Weisberg, Daniel, et al. (June 8, 2009). The Widget Effect, Retrieved from http://widgeteffect.org

46. Dillon, Sam (May 21, 2011). Behind Grass-Roots School Advocacy, Bill Gates, *New York Times*. Retrieved from http://www.nytimes.com/2011/05/22/education/22gates.html

47. Brennan, Skinner (Apr. 16, 2012). Schools fight dominates record spending on lobbying, *The New York World*. Retrieved from http://www.thenewyorkworld.com/2012/04/16/schools-fight-dominates-record-spending-on-lobbying/

48. Layton, Lyndsey (July 29, 2012). Is a Charter School Chain Called Rocketship Ready to Soar across America? *Washington Post*. Retrieved from http://www.washingtonpost.com/local/education/is-a-charter-school-chain-called-rocketship-ready-to-soar-across-america/2012/07/29/gJQASrShIX_story.html

49. Hawkins, Beth (Mar. 26, 2012). ALEC and corporate fingerprints are all over national push for online learning," *Minneapolis Post*. Retrieved from http://www.minnpost.com/learning-curve/2012/03/alec-and-corporate-fingerprints-are-all-over-national-push-online-learning

50. Pearson (Nov. 19, 2010). Project Turnaround – North Carolina. Retrieved from http://www.pearsonschool.com/index.cfm?locator=PS11Ay

51. Pearson 2013 Annual Reports and Accounts. Our performance, 2013 overview, Retrieved July 25, 2014, from http://www.pearson.com/content/dam/pearson-corporate/files/annual-reports/ar2013/03-financial-performance-ar2013.pdf

52. Gewertz, Catherine (Apr. 27, 2011). Gates, Pearson Partner to Craft Common Core Curricula, *Education Week*. Retrieved from http://www.edweek.org/ew/articles/2011/04/27/30pearson.h30.html

53. Mencimer, Stephanie (Sep. 23, 2011). Fox in the Schoolhouse: Rupert Burdoch Wants to Teach Your Kids! *Mother Jones*. Retrieved from http://motherjones.com/politics/2011/09/rupert-murdoch-news-corp-wireless-generation-education

54. *Education Week*/Editorial Projects in Education. Philanthropy, Retrieved July 25, 2014, from http://www.edweek.org/info/about/philanthropy.html?intc=thed

55. Learning Matters, Our Funders, Retrieved July 25, 2014, from http://learningmatters.tv/blog/about-us/funders/83/

56. Pelto, Jonathan (Apr. 16, 2012). How education sausage gets made: The story behind a

reform story, *Washington Post Answer Sheet*. Retrieved from http://www.washingtonpost.com/blogs/answer-sheet/post/how-ducation-sausage-gets-made-the-story-behind-a-reform-story/2012/04/15/gIQAWLkKKT_blog.html

57. Sinclair, Upton (1934). *I, Candidate for Governor: And How I Got Licked,* University of California Press, http://www.amazon.com/Candidate-Governor-And-How-Licked/dp/0520081986

58. Shaw, Linda (June 8, 2013). Gates Foundation looking to make nice with teachers, *Seattle Times*. Retrieved from http://seattletimes.com/html/education/2021149398_gatesfoundationteachersxml.html

59. Teachers' Letters to Bill Gates web site. Retrieved July 25, 2014, from http://teachersletterstobillgates.com/

60. Teachers' Letters to Bill Gates Facebook page. Retrieved July 25, 2014, from https://www.facebook.com/TeachersLetters2gates?ref=hl

61. Teachers' Letters to Bill Gates Twitter. Retrieved July 25, 2014, from https://twitter.com/TsLetters2gates

62. Parry, Mark, Field, Kelly, & Supiano, Becky (July 14, 2013). The Gates Effect, *The Chronicle of Higher Education*. Retrieved from http://chronicle.com/article/The-Gates-Effect/140323/

63. Gates quote is from the article cited in Reference 62.

64. Cody, Anthony (July 18, 2012). Virtual Schools, Real Profits, Troubling Results, *Education Week/Teacher*. Retrieved from http://blogs.edweek.org/teachers/living-in-dialogue/2012/07/virtual_schools_real_profits_t.html

65. Parr, Chris (May 10, 2013). Not Staying the Course, *Inside Higher Ed*. Retrieved from http://www.insidehighered.com/news/2013/05/10/new-study-low-mooc-completion-rates

66. Di, Xu, & Shanna Smith Jaggers (Feb. 2013). Adaptability to Online Learning: Differences Across Types of Students and Academic Subject Areas, *Teachers College*. Retrieved from http://ccrc.tc.columbia.edu/publications/adaptability-to-online-learning.html

67. Rooks, Noliwe (July 30, 2012). Why the Online Education Craze Will Leave Many Students Behind, *Time*. Retrieved from http://ideas.time.com/2012/07/30/why-online-education-will-leave-many-students-behind/

68. Bureau of Labor Statistics (Dec. 10, 2009). Occupational employment projections to 2018. Retrieved from http://www.bls.gov/opub/mlr/2009/11/art5full.pdf

69. Shierholz, Heidi (Jan. 23, 2014). Is There Really a Shortage of Skilled Workers? *Economic Policy Institute*. Retrieved from http://www.epi.org/publication/shortage-skilled-workers/

70. Gates, Bill (Feb. 28, 2011). Flip the Curve in Education Spending, speech to the National Governor's Association. [Video file]. Retrieved from: http://www.youtube.com/watch?v=pkaCx0OflKw

71. Buchheit, Paul (July 8, 2013). Four Contemptible Examples of Corporate Tax Avoidance, *Common Dreams*. Retrieved from https://www.commondreams.org/view/2013/07/08

72. Buchheit, Paul (June 17, 2013). Why Our Schools Are Broke, Five Years of Corporate Tax Avoidance, *Buzzflash*. Retrieved from http://www.truth-out.org/buzzflash/commentary/item/18030-why-our-schools-are-broke-five-years-of-corporate-state-tax-avoidance

73. Blodget, Henry (June 22, 2012). Corporate Profits Just Hit an All-Time High, Wages Hit an All-Time Low, *Business Insider*. Retrieved from http://www.businessinsider.com/corporate-profits-just-hit-an-all-time-high-wages-just-hit-an-all-time-low-2012-6

74. Cowgill, Matt (Feb. 13, 2013). How does Australia's minimum wage compare?, *We are all dead*. Retrieved from http://mattcowgill.wordpress.com/2013/02/13/australian-minimum-wages/

75. ASCD Smartbrief. Retrieved July 31, 2014, from http://www.smartbrief.com/industry/educational-leadership

76. Carter, Gene (May 5, 2010). *ASCD* Works with CCSSO and NGA on Common Core State Standards Initiative, *ASCD* press release. Retrieved from http://www.ascd.org/news-media/Press-Room/News-Releases/Common-Core-State-Standards-Statement.aspx

77. Gates Foundation (Feb. 2011). How We Work, Association for Supervision and Curriculum Development. Retrieved from http://www.gatesfoundation.org/How-We-Work/Quick-Links/Grants-Database/Grants/2011/02/OPP1030339

78. Gates Foundation (July, 2013). How We Work, Association for Supervision and Curriculum Development, *ASCD* press release. Retrieved from http://www.gatesfoundation.org/How-We-Work/Quick-Links/Grants-Database/Grants/2013/07/OPP1093511

79. Carter, Gene (Sep. 21, 2010). *ASCD* Responds to Oprah Winfrey Show's *Waiting for Superman* Episode. Retrieved from http://www.ascd.org/news-media/Press-Room/News-Releases/ASCD-Responds-to-Oprah-Winfrey-Show.aspx

80. Abrams, Madeus (Nov. 2003). The Lessons of High Stakes Testing, *Educational Leadership*. Retrieved from http://www.ascd.org/publications/educational_leadership/nov03/vol61/num03/The_Lessons_of_High-Stakes_Testing.aspx

81. Cody, Anthony (Oct. 2013). Two Ways to Lead, Educational Leadership. Retrieved from http://www.ascd.org/publications/educational-leadership/oct13/vol71/num02/Two-Ways-to-Lead.aspx

82. *ASCD* Policy Points (Oct. 2013). Common Core State Standards: Myths and Facts. Retrieved from http://www.ascd.org/ASCD/pdf/siteASCD/publications/policypoints/PolicyPoints_Common_Core_State_Standards.pdf

83. Shanahan, Timothy (Dec. 2012/Jan. 2013). The Common Core Ate My Baby and Other Urban Legends, *Educational Leadership*, Retrieved from http://www.ascd.org/publications/educational-leadership/dec12/vol70/num04/The-Common-Core-Ate-My-Baby-and-Other-Urban-Legends.aspx

84. Loveless, Tom (Dec. 2012/Jan. 2013). Commentary/ The Common Core Initiative: What Are the Chances of Success? *Educational Leadership*. Retrieved from http://www.ascd.org/publications/educational-leadership/dec12/vol70/num04/The-Common-Core-Initiative@-What-Are-the-Chances-of-Success%C2%A2.aspx

85. *ASCD*, LILA 2014 Agenda. Retrieved July 25, 2014, from http://www.ascd.org/conferences/LILA/LILA-agenda.aspx

86. Hess, Rick, Rick Hess Straight Up, *Education Week*. Retrieved July 25, 2014, from http://blogs.edweek.org/edweek/rick_hess_straight_up/

87. Hess, Rick (Sep. 18, 2013). Douglas County, The Most Interesting School District in America?" *Education Week*. Retrieved from http://blogs.edweek.org/edweek/rick_hess_straight_up/2013/09/douglas_county_the_most_interesting_school_district_in_america.html

88. Reuter, Jane (Dec. 9, 2013). Hearing reveals actions before school board election, *Castle Rock News-Press*. Retrieved from http://castlerocknewspress.net/stories/Hearing-reveals-actions-before-school-election,6856?

89. *ASCD*, (2013). Legislative Agenda. Retrieved from http://www.wsascd.org/downloads/ASCD_Resources/2013LegAgenda.pdf

90. Gallegos, Demetria (Feb. 24, 2012). Livechat: Michelle Rhee & Teacher Ratings, *Wall Street Journal*. Retrieved from http://blogs.wsj.com/metropolis/2012/02/24/live-chat-michelle-rhee-on-teacher-performance-ratings-monday-feb-27-at-1-p-m-est/

91. Cody, Anthony (Oct. 16, 2013). Process Matters in a Democracy: Common Core Fails the Test, *Education Week/Teacher*. Retrieved from http://blogs.edweek.org/teachers/living-in-dialogue/2013/10/process_matters_in_a_democracy.html

92. Boggioni, Tom (Feb. 14, 2014). Billionaire Tom Perkins's Voting Rights Act: 'pay $1 million in taxes,' get '1 million votes,' *The Raw Story*. Retrieved from http://www.rawstory.com/rs/2014/02/14/billionaire-tom-perkinss-voting-rights-act-pay-1-million-in-taxes-get-1-million-votes/

93. Gates, Bill (Feb. 12, 2014). Bill Gates: Commend Common Core, *USA Today*. Retrieved from http://www.usatoday.com/story/opinion/2014/02/11/bill-melinda-gates-common-core-education-column/5404469/

94. Cody, Anthony (July 6, 2009). The Secret Sixty Prepare to Write Standards for 50 Million, *Education Week/Teacher*. Retrieved from http://blogs.edweek.org/teachers/living-in-

dialogue/2009/07/national_standards_process_ign.html

95. Gates, Bill (July 21, 2009). Bill Gates - National Conference of State Legislatures. Retrieved from http://www.gatesfoundation.org/media-center/speeches/2009/07/bill-gates-national-conference-of-state-legislatures-ncsl

96. Thompson, John (Feb. 13, 2014). Vergara Show Trial Highlights Gates Foundation Snake Oil, *Education Week/Teacher*. Retrieved from http://blogs.edweek.org/teachers/living-in-dialogue/2014/02/vergara_show_trial.html

97. Cody, Anthony (May 23, 2013). Chicago: Time to End the Billionaires' Experiments with Mayoral Control? *Education Week/Teacher*. Retrieved from http://blogs.edweek.org/teachers/living-in-dialogue/2013/05/chicago_has_the_billionaires_e.html

98. Weiss, Elaine and Long, Don (Apr. 18, 2013). Market-oriented Education Reforms' Rhetoric Trumps Reality, *Broader Bolder Approach to Education*. Retrieved from http://www.boldapproach.org/rhetoric-trumps-reality

99. Sirota, David (Feb. 12, 2014). The Wolf of Sesame Street: Revealing the secret corruption inside PBS' news division, *Pando Daily*, Retrieved from http://pando.com/2014/02/12/the-wolf-of-sesame-street-revealing-the-secret-corruption-inside-pbss-news-division/

100. Salmon, Felix (Feb. 16, 2014). How should John Arnold approach pension reform? *Reuters*. Retrieved from http://blogs.reuters.com/felix-salmon/2014/02/15/how-should-john-arnold-approach-pension-reform/

101. Educators 4 Excellence, A Declaration of Teachers' Principles and Beliefs. Retrieved July 25, 2014, from http://educators4excellence.zissousecure.com/register

102. National Board of Professional Teaching Standards, Teaching and Learning 2014. Retrieved July 25, 2014, from http://www.teachinglearning2014.org/

103. Gates Foundation (May, 2010). How We Work, National Board for Professional Teaching Standards. Retrieved from http://www.gatesfoundation.org/How-We-Work/Quick-Links/Grants-Database/Grants/2010/05/OPP1016625

104. Gates Foundation (July, 2013). How We Work, National Board for Professional Teaching Standards. Retrieved from http://www.gatesfoundation.org/How-We-Work/Quick-Links/Grants-Database/Grants/2013/07/OPP1088311

105. Duncan, Arne (March 14, 2014). Teach to Lead: Advancing Teacher Leadership, Speech to NBPTS Conference. Retrieved from http://www.ed.gov/news/speeches/teach-lead-advancing-teacher-leadership

106. Duncan, Arne (Feb. 15, 2012). Teachers get R-E-S-P-E-C-T, Remarks at a Teacher Town Hall. Retrieved from http://www.ed.gov/news/speeches/teachers-get-r-e-s-p-e-c-t

107. Layton, Lyndsey (Mar. 14, 2014). Bill Gates calls on teachers to defend Common Core, *Washington Post*. Retrieved from http://www.washingtonpost.com/local/education/bill-gates-calls-on-teachers-to-defend-common-core/2014/03/14/395b130a-aafa-11e3-98f6-8e3c562f9996_story.html

108. Cody, Anthony (July 6, 2009). Secret Sixty Prepare to Draft Standards for 50 Million, *Education Week/Teacher*. Retrieved from http://blogs.edweek.org/teachers/living-in-dialogue/2009/07/national_standards_process_ign.html

109. Gates Foundation (July, 2013). How We Work, National Board for Professional Teaching Standards. Retrieved from http://www.gatesfoundation.org/How-We-Work/Quick-Links/Grants-Database/Grants/2013/07/OPP1088311

110. Gates, Bill & Melinda (Oct. 22, 2011). Grading the Teachers, *Wall Street Journal*. Retrieved from http://online.wsj.com/article/SB10001424052970204485304576641123767006518.html

111. Gates, Bill (Nov. 19, 2010). Bill Gates: Council of Chief State School Officers, Retrieved from http://www.gatesfoundation.org/media-center/speeches/2010/11/bill-gates-council-of-chief-state-school-officers

112. Layton, Lyndsey (Mar. 14, 2014). Bill Gates calls on teachers to defend Common Core, *Washington Post*. Retrieved from http://www.washingtonpost.com/local/education/bill-gates-calls-

on-teachers-to-defend-common-core/2014/03/14/395b130a-aafa-11e3-98f6-8e3c562f9996_story.html

113. Educators 4 Excellence, A Declaration of Teachers' Principles and Beliefs. Retrieved July 29, 2014, from http://educators4excellence.zissousecure.com/register

114. King, Martin Luther, Jr., (1967).*Where Do We Go From Here? Chaos or Community?* New York: Harper & Row

115. Impatient Optimists blog. Retrieved July 29, 2014, from http://www.impatientoptimists.org/

116. Weisberg, Daniel, et al (June 8, 2009). The Widget Effect, Retrieved from http://widgeteffect.org

117. The Shocking State of Our Schools (Sept. 20, 2010). *Oprah.com.* Retrieved from: http://www.oprah.com/oprahshow/The-Shocking-State-of-Our-Schools

118. Cody, Anthony (May 1, 2012). Teacher Research Transforms a School in Oakland, *Education Week/Teacher.* Retrieved from http://blogs.edweek.org/teachers/living-in-dialogue/2012/05/teacher_research_transforms_a_.html

119. Simmons, Aija (April 30, 2012). Getting Smarter through Teacher Research. [Video file]. Retrieved from http://www.youtube.com/watch?v=Viq8UVtsxMw

120. Mills Teacher Scholars. Retrieved July 29, 2014, from http://millsscholars.org/

121. Cody, Anthony (Oct. 12, 2011). Improving Teaching 101: Teacher Action Research, *Education Week/Teacher.* Retrieved from http://blogs.edweek.org/teachers/living-in-dialogue/2011/10/improving_teaching_101_collabo.html

122. Cody, Anthony (Oct. 25, 2011). Lesson Study Works! An Interview with Dr. Catherine Lewis, *Education Week/Teacher.* Retrieved from http://blogs.edweek.org/teachers/living-in-dialogue/2011/10/lesson_study_works.html

123. Cody, Anthony (Dec. 20, 2012). Teachers' Union Leading School Reform? Impossible! *Education Week/Teacher.* Retrieved from http://blogs.edweek.org/teachers/living-in-dialogue/2010/12/teachers_union_leading_school.html

124. Cody, Anthony (Jan. 30, 2011). TeamScience Tames Teacher Turnover in Oakland, *Education Week/Teacher.* Retrieved from http://blogs.edweek.org/teachers/living-in-dialogue/2011/01/teamscience_tames_teacher_turn.html

125. Donaldson, Morgaen L. and Johnson, Susan Moore (Oct. 4, 2011). TFA Teachers, How Long Do They Teach? Why Do They Leave? *Education Week.* Retrieved from http://www.edweek.org/ew/articles/2011/10/04/kappan_donaldson.html?intc=mcs

126. Sawchuk, Stephen (March 21, 2012). Teacher Turnover Affects All Students' Achievement, Study Indicates. *Education Week Teacher Beat* blog. Retrieved from http://blogs.edweek.org/edweek/teacherbeat/2012/03/

127. UTR United. Retrieved July 29, 2014, from http://www.utrunited.org/

128. Cody, Anthony (Mar. 10, 2012).Teacher Evaluation: Should We Look at Evidence of Learning? *Education Week/Teacher.* Retrieved from http://blogs.edweek.org/teachers/living-in-dialogue/2012/03/vam_has_driven_data_off_a_clif.html

129. Downey, Maureen (July 12, 2012). Bill Gates in Atlanta: Don't rush teacher evaluations. Do it right, *AJC.Com, Get Schooled* blog. Retrieved from http://blogs.ajc.com/get-schooled-blog/2012/07/12/bill-gates-in-atlanta-dont-rush-teacher-evaluations-do-it-right/?cxntfid=blogs_get_schooled_blog

130. Accomplished California Teachers, (2010). A Quality Teacher in Every Classroom, http://nbrc.stanford.edu/sites/default/files/ACT-a quality teacher in every classroom_0.pdf

131. Scott, Irvin (July 30, 2012). The Gates Foundation Responds: How do we Build the Teaching Profession, *Education Week/Teacher.* Retrieved from http://blogs.edweek.org/teachers/living-in-dialogue/2012/07/a_gates_foundation_response_ho.html. Also published at Impatient Optimists, Retrieved from http://www.impatientoptimists.org/Posts/2012/07/A-Response-to--How-Do-We-Build-the-Teaching-Profession

132. Phillips, Vicki (Aug. 7, 2012). A Dialogue: How Do We Consider Evidence of Student

Learning in Teacher Evaluation? *Impatient Optimists*,. Retrieved from http://www.impatientoptimists. org/Posts/2012/08/How-Do-We-Consider-Evidence-of-Student-Learning-in-Teacher-Evaluation

133. Cody, Anthony (Sep. 28, 2010). The Media's War on Teachers, *Education Week/Teacher*. Retrieved from http://blogs.edweek.org/teachers/living-in-dialogue/2010/09/the_medias_war_ on_teachers.html

134. Bill and Melinda Gates Foundation (Nov. 2011). Foundation Commits $335 Million to Promote Effective Teaching and Raise Student Achievement - Bill & Melinda Gates Foundation. Retrieved from http://www.gatesfoundation.org/Media-Center/Press-Releases/2009/11/Foundation-Commits-$335-Million-to-Promote-Effective-Teaching-and-Raise-Student-Achievement

135. Sawchuk, Stephen (Nov. 5, 2013). Gates Foundation Places Big Bet on Teacher Agenda," *Education Week*. Retrieved from http://www.edweek.org/ew/articles/2013/11/06/11gates_ep.h33.html

136. Smith, Morgan (July 28, 2012). A Serious Design Flaw is Suspected in State Tests, *New York Times*, Retrieved from http://www.nytimes.com/2012/07/29/education/texas-studies-suggest-test-design-flaw-in-taks.html

137. Rebora, Anthony (Mar. 20, 2012). Survey: Teachers Place Little Value on Standardized Tests, *Education Week*. Retrieved from http://www.edweek.org/tm/articles/2012/03/20/gates.html

138. Rubinstein, Gary (June 9, 2012). Do effective teachers teach three times as much as ineffective teachers? *Gary Rubinstein's Blog*. Retrieved from http://garyrubinstein.teachforus. org/2012/06/09/do-effective-teachers-teach-three-times-as-much-as-ineffective-teachers/

139. Glass, Gene V. (Mar. 15, 2012). Eric Hanushek Testifies in School Finance Cases, *Education in Two Worlds* blog. Retrieved from http://ed2worlds.blogspot.com/2012/03/eric-hanushek-testifies-in-school.html

140. Postal, Leslie (July 13, 2012). Teachers: New evaluation system 'artificial,' 'frustrating,' 'humiliating,' *Orlando Sentinel*. Retrieved from http://articles.orlandosentinel.com/2012-07-13/ features/os-florida-teacher-evaluations-20120713_1_new-teacher-evaluations-evaluation-plan-teacher-merit-pay-law

141. NCTQ, All Reports. Retrieved July 30, 2014, from http://www.nctq.org/reports.do

142. Data Quality Council, States' Unique Role. Retrieved July 30, 2014, from http://www. dataqualitycampaign.org/why-education-data/states-unique-role/

143. Haertel, Edward (Mar. 22, 2013). Reliability and Validity of Inferences About Teachers Based on Student Test Scores, *ETS*, Retrieved from https://www.ets.org/Media/Research/pdf/ PICANG14.pdf

144. Orfield, Gary, et al (May 15, 2014). Brown at 60, Great Progress, a Long Retreat, and an Uncertain Future," Retrieved from http://civilrightsproject.ucla.edu/research/k-12-education/ integration-and-diversity/brown-at-60-great-progress-a-long-retreat-and-an-uncertain-future/ Brown-at-60-051814.pdf

145. Rothstein, Richard (2008). *Grading Education: Getting Accountability Right*, Economic Policy Institute, http://www.epi.org/publication/books_grading_education/

146. Gates, Bill (July 12, 2012) Bill Gates in Atlanta: Don't rush teacher evaluations. Do it right, *Atlanta Journal Constitution*,. Retrieved from http://www.ajc.com/get-schooled-blog/2012/07/12/ bill-gates-in-atlanta-dont-rush-teacher-evaluations-do-it-right/

147. Darling-Hammond, Linda (Mar. 5, 2012). Value-Added Evaluation Hurts Teaching, *Education Week*. Retrieved from http://www.edweek.org/ew/articles/2012/03/05/24darlinghamm ond_ep.h31.html

148. Pink, Daniel (2009). Retrieved from *Drive: The Surprising Truth About What Motivates Us*. Riverhead Books, New York. http://www.danpink.com/books/drive/

149. Black, Paul & Wiliam, Dylan (Oct. 1998). Inside the Black Box: Raising Standards Through Assessment, *Phi Delta Kappan*. Retrieved from http://www.setda.org/toolkit/nlitoolkit2006/data/ Data_InsideBlackBox.pdf

150. Downey, Maureen (July 12, 2012). Bill Gates in Atlanta: Don't rush teacher evaluations. Do it right, *AJC.Com, Get Schooled blog*. Retrieved from http://blogs.ajc.com/get-schooled-

blog/2012/07/12/bill-gates-in-atlanta-dont-rush-teacher-evaluations-do-it-right/?cxntfid=blogs_get_schooled_blog

151. Darling-Hammond, Linda, et al, (2012). Creating a Comprehensive System for Evaluating and Supporting Effective Teaching. Retrieved from https://edpolicy.stanford.edu/sites/default/files/publications/creating-comprehensive-system-evaluating-and-supporting-effective-teaching.pdf

152. Ewing, John (May, 2011). Mathematical Intimidation: Driven by the Data, *Notices of the AMS*. Retrieved from http://www.ams.org/notices/201105/rtx110500667p.pdf

153. Haertel, Edward, et al (Sep. 14, 2011). Getting Teacher Evaluation Right: A Background Paper for Policymakers. Retrieved from http://www.aera.net/Portals/38/docs/News_Media/AERABriefings/Hill Brief - Teacher Eval 2011/GettingTeacherEvaluationRightBackgroundPaper%281%29.pdf

154. American Statistical Association (Apr. 8, 2014). ASA Statement on Using Value-Added Models for Educational Assessment. Retrieved from http://www.amstat.org/policy/pdfs/ASA_VAM_Statement.pdf

155. Casey, Leo (Feb. 28, 2012). The True Story of Pascale Mauclair, *EdWize*. Retrieved from http://www.edwize.org/the-true-story-of-pascale-mauclair

156. Tucker, Jill (Aug. 25, 2007). Children who survive urban warfare suffer from PTSD, too, *San Francisco Chronicle*. Retrieved from http://articles.sfgate.com/2007-08-26/news/17256954_1_ptsd-war-zone-post-traumatic-stress-disorder

157. Fox, Maggie (June 14, 2010). Murder rates affect IQ tests scores: study, *Reuters*. Retrieved from http://www.reuters.com/article/2010/06/14/us-violence-children-idUSTRE65D5VW20100614

158. Oakland Tribune (April 4, 2013). Info Graphic: Oakland Homicides 2012 Map. Retrieved from http://www.insidebayarea.com/crime/ci_22942237

159. Center on the Developing Child, Five Numbers to Remember About Early Childhood Development. Retrieved July 30, 2014 from http://developingchild.harvard.edu/index.php/download_file/-/view/949/

160. Anna E. Casey Foundation, (2012). 2012 Kids Count Data Book. Retrieved from http://datacenter.kidscount.org/databook/2012/#downloadbook

161. Shanks, Trina & Robinson, Christine (2012). Assets, Economic Opportunity, and Toxic Stress: A Framework for Understanding Child and Educational Outcomes. Retrieved from http://csd.wustl.edu/Publications/Documents/WP12-22.pdf

162. Coté, John (Aug. 26, 2009). Oakland apartments condemned, residents out, *San Francisco Chronicle*. Retrieved from http://www.sfgate.com/bayarea/article/Oakland-apartments-condemned-residents-out-3220385.php

163. Ed Data Express. Retrieved July 30, 2014, from http://eddataexpress.ed.gov

164. No Kid Hungry, Hunger Facts. Retrieved July 30, 2014, from http://www.nokidhungry.org/problem/hunger-facts

165. Seidel, Jeff (Dec. 8, 2011). Michigan's homeless students: Foreclosure crisis takes toll on 31,000 kids, *Detroit Free Press*. Retrieved from http://www.freep.com/article/20111218/NEWS06/112180464/Michigan-s-homeless-students

166. Marder, Michael (April 29, 2014). Education and Poverty. Image used with permission. http://prezi.com/4zetuvjyy8je/education-and-poverty/

167. Hanushek, Eric (Sep. 27, 2010). Policies: Kyla Johnson-Trammel, David Plank, Senator Carol Liu, Richard Rothstein, Eric Hanushek, [Video file]. (transcribed from video). https://www.youtube.com/watch?v=pSpq3K_9Cyw

168. Brandenburg, Guy (May 8, 2014). Just how flat ARE those 12th grade NAEP scores? Retrieved from http://gfbrandenburg.wordpress.com/2014/05/08/just-how-flat-are-those-12th-grade-naep-scores/

169. Sahlberg, Pasi (2011). *Finnish Lessons: What Can the World Learn from Educational Change in Finland?* Teachers College Press. Retrieved from http://www.finnishlessons.com/

170. Adelman, Howard & Taylor, Linda (Aug. 2, 2012). Learning Supports, the Missing Component in School Improvement, *Education Week/Teacher*. Retrieved from http://blogs.edweek.

org/teachers/living-in-dialogue/2012/08/learning_supports_the_missing_.html

171. Broader, Bolder Approach (2011). A Broader, Bolder Approach to Education,. Retrieved from http://www.epi.org/files/2011/bold_approach_full_statement-3.pdf

172. Opportunity to Learn Campaign. Retrieved July 30, 2014, http://www.otlcampaign.org/

173. Rothstein, Richard (Feb. 3, 2012). Racial segregation continues, and even intensifies, *Economic Policy Institute*, Retrieved from http://www.epi.org/publication/racial-segregation-continues-intensifies/

174. Garofalo, Pat (July 17, 2012). Walmart Heirs Have As Much Wealth As Bottom 40% of Americans Combined. *Think Progress*. Retrieved from http://thinkprogress.org/economy/2012/07/17/534591/walmart-heirs-wealth-combined/

175. Martens, Pam (July 21, 2012). How Wall Street Gutted Our Schools and Cities, *Reader Supported News*. Retrieved from http://readersupportednews.org/opinion2/279-82/12546-how-wall-street-gutted-our-schools-and-cities

176. Kozol, Jonathan (1991). *Savage Inequalities*, Crown Publishing, New York.

177. Sauter, Michael B., et al (June 6, 2012). America's Richest School Districts, *24/7 Wall St.* Retrieved from http://247wallst.com/2012/06/06/americas-richest-school-districts/

178. Lakeside School, About us. Retrieved July 30, 2014, from http://www.lakesideschool.org/aboutus

179. Williams, Chris (Aug. 20, 2012). The Gates Foundation Responds: Poverty Does Matter, But It Is Not Destiny, *Education Week/Teacher*, Retrieved from http://blogs.edweek.org/teachers/living-in-dialogue/2012/08/the_gates_foundation_responds_.html Also retrieved from *Impatient Optimists*: http://www.impatientoptimists.org/Posts/2012/08/Poverty-Does-MatterBut-It-Is-Not-Destiny

180. Scott, Irvin (Aug. 28, 2012). The Gates Foundation Writes: K12 Education: An Opportunity Catalyst, *Education Week/Teacher*. Retrieved from http://blogs.edweek.org/teachers/living-in-dialogue/2012/08/the_gates_foundation_writes_k-.htmlAlso retrieved from http://www.impatientoptimists.org/Posts/2012/08/K12-Education-An-Opportunity-Catalyst

181. Shepherd, Robert (Aug. 25, 2012). Finding the Genius in Every Child, *Diane Ravitch's blog*. Retrieved from http://dianeravitch.net/2012/08/25/finding-the-genius-in-every-child/

182. Burris, Carol & Garrity, Delia (2008). *Detracking for Excellence and Equity*, Association for Supervision & Curriculum Development. Retrieved from http://www.ascd.org/publications/books/108013/chapters/What-Tracking-Is-and-How-to-Start-Dismantling-It.aspx

183. Block, Melissa (Apr. 24, 2012). Student Loan Debt Now Exceeds One Trillion Dollars, *NPR, All Things Considered*. Retrieved from http://www.npr.org/2012/04/24/151305380/student-loan-debt-exceeds-one-trillion-dollars

184. Martin, Andrew & Lehren, Andrew (May 12, 2012). A generation hobbled by the soaring cost of college, *New York Times*. Retrieved from http://www.nytimes.com/2012/05/13/business/student-loans-weighing-down-a-generation-with-heavy-debt.html?pagewanted=all

185. Turl, Adam (Aug. 27, 2012). College Students are Homeless and Hungry, and Corporate America is Trying to Exploit Them, *Alternet*. Retrieved from http://www.alternet.org/homeless-and-hungry-college

186. Heenan, Adam (Aug. 24, 2012). Email correspondence.

187. Cody, Anthony (Nov. 15, 2010). Doug Christensen: Local Initiative, Self-determination and Leadership are the ONLY Thing, *Education Week/Teacher*. Retrieved from http://blogs.edweek.org/teachers/living-in-dialogue/2010/11/doug_christensen_local_initiat.html

188. ACT (July 2, 2012). ACT to Launch Next Generation College and Career Readiness Assessment System Aligned To Common Core State Standards and More, Retrieved from http://www.act.org/newsroom/releases/view.php?lang=english&p=2355

189. Almon, Joan & Miller, Edward (Nov. 2011). The Crisis in Early Education, *Alliance for Childhood*. Retrieved from http://www.allianceforchildhood.org/sites/allianceforchildhood.org/files/file/crisis_in_early_ed.pdf

190. Zhao, Yong (Aug. 16, 2012). Double-Think: The Creativity-Testing Conflict, *Yong Zhao blog*.

Retrieved from http://zhaolearning.com/2012/08/16/doublethink-the-creativity-testing-conflict/

191. Duncan, Arne (Sep. 2, 2010). Beyond the Bubble Tests: The Next Generation of Assessments, Retrieved from http://www.ed.gov/news/speeches/beyond-bubble-tests-next-generation-assessments-secretary-arne-duncans-remarks-state-l

192. Merrow, John (Aug. 28, 2012). A Polarized Education System, *Taking Note blog*, Retrieved from http://takingnote.learningmatters.tv/?p=5885

193. Bush, Jeb (Aug. 30, 2012). Jeb Bush RNC Speech, *Politico*. Retrieved from http://www.politico.com/news/stories/0812/80486.html

194. Wallis, Claudia (June 8, 2008). No Child Left Behind: Doomed to Fail? *Time*, Retrieved from http://www.time.com/time/nation/article/0,8599,1812758,00.html

195. Thomas B. Fordham Institute Five-Year Report, 1997 – 2001 (May 2002). Retrieved from http://www.edexcellencemedia.net/publications/2002/200205_tbfffiveyear/report.pdf

196. Zhao, Yong (Aug. 14, 2009). Demystifying the Link between Performance on International Tests and Economic Competitiveness, *Yong Zhao blog*. Retrieved from http://zhaolearning.com/2009/08/14/demystifying-the-link-between-performance-on-international-tests-and-economic-competitiveness/

197. Tomassini, Jason (Aug. 7, 2012). Business Opportunities Seen in New Tests, Low Scores, *Education Week*. Retrieved from http://blogs.edweek.org/edweek/marketplacek12/2012/08/as_assessments_change_and_scores_drop_business_opportunities_arise.html

198. The Parthenon Group (July 26, 2012). *Parthenon Perspectives: Balancing Opportunity and Risk in North American K-12 Publishing*. Retrieved from http://blogs.edweek.org/edweek/marketplacek12/120726 Parthenon Perspectives_Balancing Opportunity and Risk in K12.pdf

199. Phillips, Vicki (Aug. 3, 2011). Shared Tools for Teachers? There's an App for That! *Impatient Optimists blog*, Retrieved from http://www.impatientoptimists.org/Posts/2011/08/Shared-Tools-for-Teachers

200. Gates Foundation (April, 2011). Gates Foundation Announces Portfolio of Innovative Grants to Develop New Teaching and Learning Tools that Support Teachers and Help Students. http://www.gatesfoundation.org/Media-Center/Press-Releases/2011/04/gates-Foundation-Announces-Portfolio-of-Innovative-Grants-to-Develop-New-Teaching-and-Learning-Tools-that-Support-Teachers-and-Help-Students

201. Gates, Bill (January, 2009). Annual Letter 2009. Retrieved from http://www.gatesfoundation.org/who-we-are/resources-and-media/annual-letters-list/annual-letter-2009

202. Michels, Patrick (Feb. 29, 2012). Austin ISD Enters Gates-Funded Truce with Charters, *Texas Observer*. Retrieved from http://www.texasobserver.org/austin-isd-enters-gates-funded-truce-with-charters/

203. CREDO (2009). Multiple Choice: Charter School Performance in 16 States. Retrieved from http://credo.stanford.edu/reports/MULTIPLE_CHOICE_EXECUTIVE SUMMARY.pdf

204. Capital Roundtable (July 26, 2012). Private Equity Investing In For-Profit Education Companies. Retrieved from http://www.capitalroundtable.com/masterclass/For-Profit-Education-Private-Equity-Conference-2012.html

205. Hernandez, Javier (Dec. 12, 2013. Educational Publisher's Charity Accused of Seeking Profits, Will Pay Millions, *New York Times*, Retrieved from http://www.nytimes.com/2013/12/13/nyregion/educational-publishers-charity-accused-of-seeking-profits-will-pay-millions.html

206. Garcia-Roberts, Gus (June 23, 2011). McKay scholarship program sparks a cottage industry of fraud and chaos, *Miami NewTimes News*. Retrieved from http://www.miaminewtimes.com/2011-06-23/news/mckay-scholarship-program-sparks-a-cottage-industry-of-fraud-and-chaos/

207. Hoag, Christina (Aug. 19, 2012). Charter schools leave special-needs kids behind, *Davis Enterprise*. Retrieved from http://www.davisenterprise.com/local-news/associated-press/charter-schools-leave-special-needs-kids-behind/

208. Vasquez-Heilig, Julian (2011). Is Choice a Panacea? An Analysis of Black Secondary Student Attrition from KIPP, Other Private Charters, and Urban Districts, *Berkeley Review of Education*.

Retrieved from http://escholarship.org/uc/item/0vs9d4fr#page-2

209. Frankenberg, Erica, et al (June 26, 2012). Choice Without Equity: Charter School Segregation and the Need for Civil Rights Standards. Retrieved from http://civilrightsproject.ucla.edu/news/press-releases/research/k-12-education/integration-and-diversity/choice-without-equity-2009-report

210. Fang, Lee (Nov. 17, 2011). Selling Schools Out, *The Nation*. Retrieved from http://www.theinvestigativefund.org/investigations/corporateaccountability/1580/?page=entire

211. Woodard, Colin (Sep. 2, 2012). Special Report: The profit motive behind virtual schools in Maine, *Portland Press Herald*. Retrieved from http://www.pressherald.com/news/virtual-schools-in-maine_2012-09-02.html

212. Miron, Gary (July, 2012). Understanding and Improving Full-Time Virtual Schools. Retrieved from http://nepc.colorado.edu/files/nepc-rb-k12-miron.pdf

213. Foundation for Excellence in Education, Meet Our Donors. Retrieved July 31, 2014, from http://excelined.org/about-us/meet-our-donors/

214. Gates Foundation (June 2012). How We Work, grant: Foundation for Excellence in Education Inc. Retrieved from http://www.gatesfoundation.org/How-We-Work/Quick-Links/Grants-Database/Grants/2012/06/OPP1062620

215. Parent Revolution (Dec. 26, 2012). "Our Funders," (retrieved from the Wayback machine web archive: https://web.archive.org/web/20121226175017/http://parentrevolution.org/content/our-funders)

216. The Media Bullpen. Retrieved July 31, 2014, from http://mediabullpen.com/

217. The Mind Trust (Oct. 14, 2011). The Mind Trust Receives Grant to Expand its National Network: the Cities for Education Entrepreneurship Trust (CEE-Trust). Retrieved from http://cee-trust.org/upload/news/1014111028_CEE-Trust%20Press%20Release.pdf

218. Buzzfeed staff (Apr. 10, 2012). Gates Won't Pull ALEC Grant, *Buzzfeed*. Retrieved from http://www.buzzfeed.com/buzzfeedpolitics/gates-wont-pull-alec-grant

219. Scott, Irvin & Childress, Stacey (Sep. 13, 2012). The Gates Foundation Responds: The Role of the Marketplace in Education Reform. Retrieved from http://blogs.edweek.org/teachers/living-in-dialogue/2012/09/the_dialogue_with_the_gates_fo.html Also posted at http://www.impatientoptimists.org/Posts/2012/09/Response-to-Anthony-Cody-The-Role-of-the-Marketplace-in-Education

220. Gates, Bill (Mar. 17, 2014). Speaking Up for the Common Core, *GatesNotes*. Retrieved from http://www.gatesnotes.com/Education/Speaking-Up-for-Common-Core

221. Head, Simon (2014). *Mindless: How Smarter Machines are Making Us Dumber Humans*, Basic Books. http://www.amazon.com/Mindless-Smarter-Machines-Making-Dumber/dp/0465018440

222. Nocera, Joe (May 21, 2012). Gates Puts the Focus on Teaching, *New York Times*, Retrieved from http://www.nytimes.com/2012/05/22/opinion/nocera-gates-puts-the-focus-on-teaching.html

223. iMotions, Affectiva GSR Qsensor. Retrieved July 31, 2014, from http://imotionsglobal.com/portfolio-item/affectiva-gsr-qsensor/

224. Gates Foundation (Nov. 2011). Grants, Clemson University, (retrieved from the Wayback Machine web archive) http://web.archive.org/web/20120614175342/http://www.gatesfoundation.org/Grants-2011/Pages/Clemson-University-OPP1049604.aspx

225. Gates Foundation (Nov. 2011). How We Work, National Center on Time and Learning. Retrieved from http://www.Gatesfoundation.org/How-We-Work/Quick-Links/Grants-Database#q/k=National%20Center%20on%20Time%20and%20Learning

226. The Week Staff (Jan. 26, 2011). Cameras in the classroom: Should we film teachers at work? *The Week*, Retrieved from http://theweek.com/article/index/211430/cameras-in-the-classroom-should-we-film-teachers-at-work

227. Petrilli, Michael (Spring, 2011). Lights, Camera, Action!, *EducationNext*. Retrieved http://educationnext.org/lights-camera-action/

228. Kroll, Luisa (June 13, 2012). Gates Foundation Responds to GSR Bracelets Controversy, *Forbes*, Retrieved from http://www.forbes.com/sites/luisakroll/2012/06/13/gates-foundation-

responds-to-gsr-bracelets-controversy/

229. Pierson, Rita (May, 2013). Every kid needs a champion, *TEDTalks*. Retrieved from http://www.ted.com/talks/rita_pierson_every_kid_needs_a_champion

230. Musallam, Ramsey (Apr. 2013). 3 rules to spark learning," [Video file]. Retrieved from http://www.ted.com/talks/ramsey_musallam_3_rules_to_spark_learning

231. Samimi-Moore, Shirin (May 8, 2013). Meet five New York high school students with fascinating stories, *TED Blog*. Retrieved from http://blog.ted.com/2013/05/08/10-talks-from-inspiring-teachers-2-2/

232. Gates, Bill (May, 2013). Teachers need real feedback, [Video file]. Retrieved from http://www.ted.com/talks/bill_gates_teachers_need_real_feedback

233. Zhao, Yong (Aug. 16, 2012). Double-Think: The Creativity-Testing Conflict, *Yong Zhao blog*, Retrieved from http://zhaolearning.com/2012/08/16/doublethink-the-creativity-testing-conflict/

234. Cody, Anthony (Oct. 25, 2011). Lesson Study Works! An Interview with Dr. Catherine Lewis, *Education Week/Teacher*. Retrieved from http://blogs.edweek.org/teachers/living-in-dialogue/2011/10/lesson_study_works.html

235. Cody, Anthony (May 1, 2012). Teacher Research Transforms a School in Oakland, *Education Week/Teacher*. Retrieved from http://blogs.edweek.org/teachers/living-in-dialogue/2012/05/teacher_research_transforms_a_.html

236. Darling-Hammond, Linda, (Apr. 11, 2013). What teachers need and reformers ignore: time to collaborate, *Washington Post/Answer Sheet* blog. Retrieved from http://www.washingtonpost.com/blogs/answer-sheet/wp/2013/04/11/what-teachers-need-and-reformers-ignore-time-to-collaborate/

237. Robinson, Sir Ken (Apr. 2013). How to escape education's Death Valley, [Video file]. Retrieved from http://www.ted.com/talks/ken_robinson_how_to_escape_education_s_death_valley

238. Gates, Bill (July 28, 2009). Bill Gates at the National Conference of State Legislatures," [Video file]. Retrieved from http://www.youtube.com/watch?v=xtTK_6VKpf4#t=47

239. McRae, Phil (Apr. 29, 2013). Rebirth of the Teaching Machine through the Seduction of Data Analytics: This Time It's Personal, *for the love of learning* blog. Retrieved from http://www.joebower.org/2013/04/rebirth-of-teaching-machine-through.html?spref=tw

240. B.F. Skinner (1954). B.F. Skinner. Teaching machine and programmed learning, [Video file]. Retrieved from http://www.youtube.com/watch?v=jTH3ob1IRFo

241. U.S. Department of Education, Competency Based Education or Personalized Learning. Retrieved July 31, 2014, from http://www.ed.gov/oii-news/competency-based-learning-or-personalized-learning

242. Cody, Anthony (May 3, 2014). Computerized Grading: Purloining the Analysis, the Most Fundamental Exposition of Humanity, *Education Week/Teacher*. Retrieved from http://blogs.edweek.org/teachers/living-in-dialogue/2014/05/computerized_grading_purloinin.html

243. Perelman, Les (2014). Critique of Mark D. Shermis & Ben Hamner, Contrasting State-of-the-Art Automated Scoring of Essays: Analysis, *Journal of Writing Assessment*. Retrieved from http://journalofwritingassessment.org/article.php?article=69

244. Cody, Anthony (Feb. 5, 2013). Does the Battle in Seattle Foreshadow Trouble for the Common Core? *Education Week/Teacher*. Retrieved from http://blogs.edweek.org/teachers/living-in-dialogue/2013/02/does_the_battle_in_seattle_for.html

245. Auerbach, David (Winter, 2012). The Stupidity of Computers, *N plus 1*. Retrieved from https://nplusonemag.com/issue-13/essays/stupidity-of-computers/

246. Greene, David (Apr. 30, 2013). Invitation to a Dialogue: The Art of Teaching, *New York Times*. Retrieved from http://www.nytimes.com/2013/05/01/opinion/invitation-to-a-dialogue-the-art-of-teaching.html?_r=0

247. Providence Student Union (Apr. 30, 2013). Providence Student Union's First Annual State of the Student Address. *Diane Ravitch's blog*. Retrieved from http://dianeravitch.net/2013/04/30/dont-you-love-the-providence-student-union/

248. Grossman, Sara (July 16, 2013). Bill Gates Discusses MOOCs at Microsoft Research's Faculty

Summit, *The Chronicle of Higher Education*. Retrieved from http://chronicle.com/blogs/wiredcampus/bill-gates-discusses-moocs-at-microsoft-researchs-faculty-summit

249. Mangan, Katherine (Oct. 3, 2013). MOOCs Could Help 2-Year Colleges and Their Students, Says Bill Gates, *The Chronicle of Higher Education*, Retrieved from http://chronicle.com/article/MOOCs-Could-Help-2-Year/142123/

250. Gates Foundation, How We Work, Search Results, 'MOOC', Retrieved July 31, 2014, from http://www.gatesfoundation.org/search#q/k=mooc

251. Guzdial, Mark (Oct. 18, 2013). Results From the First-Year Course MOOCs: Not There Yet, *Communications of the ACM*. Retrieved from http://cacm.acm.org/blogs/blog-cacm/168862-results-from-the-first-year-course-moocs-not-there-yet/fulltext

252. Head, Karen (Sep. 6, 2013). Lessons Learned From a Freshman-Composition MOOC, *The Chronicle of Higher Education*, Retrieved from http://chronicle.com/blogs/wiredcampus/lessons-learned-from-a-freshman-composition-mooc/46337

253. Parr, Chris (May 10, 2013). Not Staying the Course, *Inside Higher Ed*. Retrieved from http://www.insidehighered.com/news/2013/05/10/new-study-low-mooc-completion-rates

254. Philosophy Department at San Jose State University (May 2, 2013). An Open Letter to Professor Michael Sandel From the Philosophy Department at San Jose State U., *The Chronicle of Higher Education*. Retrieved from http://chronicle.com/article/The-Document-an-Open-Letter/138937/

255. Bear, Charla (Aug. 20, 2013). San Jose State Rethinking Online Courses After Dismal Start, *KQED News*. Retrieved from http://blogs.kqed.org/newsfix/2013/08/19/a-second-look-at-massive-online-classes-after-san-joe/

256. Layton, Lyndsey (Mar. 14, 2014). Bill Gates calls on teachers to defend Common Core, *Washington Post*. Retrieved from http://www.washingtonpost.com/local/education/bill-gates-calls-on-teachers-to-defend-common-core/2014/03/14/395b130a-aafa-11e3-98f6-8e3c562f9996_story.html

257. Gates, Bill (July 11, 2012). Bill Gates: Education Commission of the United States Annual Conference. Retrieved from http://www.gatesfoundation.org/media-center/speeches/2012/07/bill-gates-education-commission-of-the-states-annual-conference

258. Kamenetz, Anya (Apr. 3, 2014). What Will Happen to 'Big Data' In Education? *MindShift*. Retrieved from http://blogs.kqed.org/mindshift/2014/04/what-will-happen-to-big-data-in-education/

259. Amplify, Tablet. Retrieved July 31, 2014, from http://www.amplify.com/tablet

260. Pearson (Feb. 20, 2014). Global Leader Pearson Creates Leading Curriculum, Apps, for Digital Learning Environments, *Digital Journal*. Retrieved from http://www.prweb.com/releases/2014/02/prweb11601976.htm

261. Herold, Benjamin (Jan. 21, 2014). Growing Pains for Rocketship's Blended Learning Juggernaut, *Education Week*, Retrieved from http://www.edweek.org/ew/articles/2014/01/21/19el-rotation.h33.html

262. Blume, Howard (Feb. 27, 2014). Former L.A. schools chief calls iPad program illegal," *Los Angeles Times*. Retrieved from http://www.latimes.com/local/lanow/la-me-ln-former-schools-chief-ipad-illegal-20140227-story.html

263. Class Size Matters, *Class Size Reduction Research*. Retrieved July 31, 2014, from http://www.classsizematters.org/research-and-links/

264. Jabr, Ferris (Apr. 11, 2013). The Reading Brain in the Digital Age: The Science of Paper vs. Screens, *Scientific American*. Retrieved from http://www.scientificamerican.com/article/reading-paper-screens/

265. Kolodny, Carina (May 6, 2014). Stephen Hawking is Terrified of Artificial Intelligence, *Huffington Post*, Retrieved from http://www.huffingtonpost.com/2014/05/05/stephen-hawking-artificial-intelligence_n_5267481.html

266. Head, Simon (2014). *Mindless: How Smarter Machines are Making Us Dumber Humans*, Basic

Books. http://www.amazon.com/Mindless-Smarter-Machines-Making-Dumber/dp/0465018440

267. Gilens, Martin and Page, Benjamin (Apr. 9, 2014). Testing Theories of American Politics: Elites, Interest Groups and Average Citizens. Retrieved from http://www.princeton.edu/~mgilens/ Gilens homepage materials/Gilens and Page/Gilens and Page 2014-Testing Theories 3-7-14.pdf

268. Head, Simon (2014). *Mindless: How Smarter Machines are Making Us Dumber Humans*, Basic Books. http://www.amazon.com/Mindless-Smarter-Machines-Making-Dumber/dp/0465018440

269. Backer, Patricia Ryaby (June 11, 1998). Scientific Management. Retrieved from http://www.engr.sjsu.edu/pabacker/scientific_mgt.htm

270. Ferreira, Jose (Nov. 3, 2012). Knewton – Education Datapalooza, [Video file]. Retrieved from http://www.youtube.com/watch?v=Lr7Z7ysDluQ

271. Layton, Lyndsey (Mar. 14, 2014). Bill Gates calls on teachers to defend Common Core, *Washington Post*. Retrieved from http://www.washingtonpost.com/local/education/bill-gates-calls-on-teachers-to-defend-common-core/2014/03/14/395b130a-aafa-11e3-98f6-8e3c562f9996_story.html

272. Rutkin, Aviva Hope (Sep. 13, 2013). Report Suggests Nearly Half of US Jobs Are Vulnerable to Computerization, *MIT Technology Review*. Retrieved from http://www.technologyreview.com/view/519241/report-suggests-nearly-half-of-us-jobs-are-vulnerable-to-computerization/

273. Sagan, Carl (1997). *Demon-Haunted World: Science as a Candle in the Dark*, Ballantine Books. http://www.amazon.com/The-Demon-Haunted-World-Science-Candle/dp/0345409469

274. Gates, Bill (Jan., 2013). Annual Letter 2013, Retrieved from http://www.gatesfoundation.org/Who-We-Are/Resources-and-Media/Annual-Letters-List/Annual-Letter-2013

275. Gates, Bill (Jan. 24, 2013). My Annual Letter: Accelerating Impact Through Measurement," *Impatient Optimists* blog. Retrieved from http://www.impatientoptimists.org/Posts/2013/01/My-Annual-Letter-Accelerating-Impact-through-Measurement

276. O'Neil, Cathy (Jan. 29, 2013). Bill Gates is naïve, data is not objective, *Mathbabe* blog. Retrieved from http://mathbabe.org/2013/01/29/bill-gates-is-naive-data-is-not-objective/

277. Rubinstein, Gary (Feb. 3, 2013). The Eagle Has Landed, *Gary Rubinstein's blog.* Retrieved from http://garyrubinstein.teachforus.org/2013/02/03/the-eagle-has-landed/

278. Sidwell Friends School, School Philosophy. Retrieved July 31, 2014, from http://www.sidwell.edu/about_sfs/school-philosophy/index.aspx

279. Lakeside School, "Academics Overview." Retrieved July 31, 2014, from http://www.lakesideschool.org/academics

280. King, Dr. Martin Luther, Jr. (Jan-Feb. 1947). *The Purpose of Education.* Retrieved from http://mlk-kpp01.stanford.edu/index.php/encyclopedia/documentsentry/doc_470200_000/

281. Gates, Bill (Jan., 2013). Annual Letter 2013. Retrieved from http://www.gatesfoundation.org/Who-We-Are/Resources-and-Media/Annual-Letters-List/Annual-Letter-2013

282. Boccanfuso, Christopher, et al (July, 2010). Ten Ways to Promote Educational Achievement Beyond the Classroom," *Research to Results Brief.* Retrieved from http://www.mentoring.org/downloads/mentoring_1263.pdf

283. Resmovits, Joy (Oct. 2, 2012). School Funding Inequity Forces Poor Districts Like Reading, Pa., to Take Huge Cuts," *Huffington Post*. Retrieved from http://www.huffingtonpost.com/2012/10/02/school-funding-reading-pennsylvania_n_1922577.html

284. Jamrisko, Michelle, & Kolet, Ilan (Aug. 15, 2012). *Bloomberg News*. Retrieved from http://www.bloomberg.com/news/2012-08-15/cost-of-college-degree-in-u-s-soars-12-fold-chart-of-the-day.html

285. Evans, Kelly (July 12, 2012). Student Debt: America's $1 Trillion Time Bomb, *CNBC*, Retrieved from http://www.cnbc.com/id/48148304

286. deParle, Jason (Dec. 22, 2012). For Poor, Leap to College Often Ends in a Hard Fall, *New York Times*. Retrieved from http://www.nytimes.com/2012/12/23/education/poor-students-struggle-as-class-plays-a-greater-role-in-success.html

287. Drum, Kevin (Jan./Feb., 2013). America's Real Criminal Element: Lead, *Mother Jones*. Retrieved from http://www.motherjones.com/environment/2013/01/lead-crime-link-gasoline

288. Cody, Anthony (Feb. 11, 2013). An Open Letter to Bill Gates: Why Not Measure This? (comment by Lisa Guernsey). Retrieved from http://blogs.edweek.org/teachers/living-in-dialogue/2013/02/an_open_letter_to_bill_gates_w.html

289. Williams, Chris (Aug. 20, 2012). Poverty Does Matter – But It Is Not Destiny, *Impatient Optimists*. Retrieved from http://www.impatientoptimists.org/Posts/2012/08/Poverty-Does-MatterBut-It-Is-Not-Destiny. Also retrieved from http://blogs.edweek.org/teachers/living-in-dialogue/2012/08/the_gates_foundation_responds_.html

290. Gates, Bill (Apr. 3, 2013). Bill Gates: A fairer way to evaluate teachers, *Washington Post*. Retrieved from http://www.washingtonpost.com/opinions/bill-gates-a-fairer-way-to-evaluate-teachers/2013/04/03/c99fd1bc-98c2-11e2-814b-063623d80a60_story.html

291. McNeil, Michele (Mar. 18, 2009). The Ed Department's Pearly 'Gates,' *Education Week*. Retrieved from http://blogs.edweek.org/edweek/campaign-k-12/2009/03/do_all_ed_dept_roads_lead_to_g.html

292. NCTQ (May, 2012). What Teacher Preparation Programs Teach About K-12 Assessment. Retrieved from http://www.nctq.org/dmsView/What_Teacher_Prep_Programs_Teach_K-12_Assessment_NCTQ_Report

293. Dillon, Sam (May 21, 2011). Behind Grass-Roots School Advocacy, Bill Gates, *New York Times*. Retrieved from http://www.nytimes.com/2011/05/22/education/22gates.html

294. The Media Bullpen. Retrieved July 31, 2014, from http://mediabullpen.com/

295. Gates Foundation, (Oct. 2011). How We Work, Center for Education Reform. Retrieved from http://www.gatesfoundation.org/How-We-Work/Quick-Links/Grants-Database/Grants/2011/10/OPP1035814

296. Ryan, Terry, (Mar. 27, 2013). Teacher Evaluation Overkill in Ohio – What about PE Teachers? *Gadfly Daily*, Retrieved from http://www.edexcellence.net/commentary/education-gadfly-daily/ohio-gadfly-daily/2013/teacher-evaluation-overkill-in-ohio-what-about-pe-teachers.html

297. Physical Education in Ohio, Retrieved July 31, 2014, from http://education.ohio.gov/GD/Templates/Pages/ODE/ODEDetail.aspx?page=3&TopicRelationID=1793&ContentID=132131&Content=139137

298. Dillon, Sam (May 21, 2011). Behind Grass-Roots School Advocacy, Bill Gates, *New York Times*. Retrieved from http://www.nytimes.com/2011/05/22/education/22gates.html

299. Senate Bill No. 1 (Feb. 16, 2011). Retrieved from http://www.in.gov/legislative/bills/2011/SB/SB0001.1.html

300. Phillips, Vicki and Weingarten, Randi (April, 2013). The Elements of a Quality Teacher Development and Evaluation System, *The New Republic*. Retrieved from http://www.aft.org/newspubs/news/2013/032513newrepublic.cfm

301. Gates, Bill (Dec. 9, 2008). Bill Gates Discusses Mayoral Control. [Video file]. Retrieved from http://www.youtube.com/watch?v=fSSYHj_6dX

302. Department of Education (June 8, 2009) States Open to Charters Start Fast in 'Race to the Top'. Retrieved from http://www2.ed.gov/news/pressreleases/2009/06/06082009a.html

303. The Shocking State of Our Schools (Sept. 20, 2010). *Oprah.com*. Retrieved from: http://www.oprah.com/oprahshow/The-Shocking-State-of-Our-Schools

304. Weiss, Elaine and Long, Don (Apr. 18, 2013). Market-oriented education reforms' rhetoric trumps reality, Broader, *Bolder Approach to Education*, Retrieved from http://www.boldapproach.org/rhetoric-trumps-reality

305. American Statistical Association (Apr. 8, 2014). ASA Statement on Using Value-Added Models for Educational Assessment. Retrieved from http://www.amstat.org/policy/pdfs/ASA_VAM_Statement.pdf

306. Haertel, et al (2011). Getting Teacher Evaluation Right: A Brief for Policymakers, *SCOPE*, https://edpolicy.stanford.edu/sites/default/files/publications/getting-teacher-evaluation-right-

challenge-policy-makers.pdf

307. Solochek, Jeff (Dec. 3, 2012). Florida's value-added model snags top Alachua teacher, *Tampa Bay Times*. Retrieved from http://www.tampabay.com/blogs/gradebook/content/floridas-value-added-model-snares-top-alachua-teacher

308. Miron, Gary (July, 2012). Understanding and Improving Full-Time Virtual Schools, Retrieved from http://nepc.colorado.edu/files/nepc-rb-k12-miron.pdf

309. Little, Darnell (Apr. 7, 2014). Charter schools show little difference in student performance, *Chicago Sun Times*. Retrieved from http://www.suntimes.com/26686762-761/a-push-for-charter-schools-but-little-difference-in-student-performance.html

310. Rotberg, Iris C. (Mar. 27, 2014). Charter Schools and the Risk of Increased Segregation, *Education Week*, Retrieved from http://www.edweek.org/ew/articles/2014/02/01/kappan_rotberg.html

311. Vasquez-Heilig, Julian (Nov. 11, 2013). Diversity is Hard: Will Charter Schools in Your Area Choose Equity? *Cloaking Inequity*. Retrieved from http://cloakinginequity.com/2013/11/11/diversity-is-hard-will-charter-schools-in-your-locale-choose-equity/

312. Xinhua (Apr. 18, 2014). Chile to end private education, *Shanghai Daily*. Retrieved from http://www.shanghaidaily.com/article/article_xinhua.aspx?id=213464

313. Pollard, Niklas (Dec. 10, 2013). Insight: Sweden rethinks pioneering school reforms, private equity under fire, *Reuters*. Retrieved from http://www.reuters.com/article/2013/12/10/us-sweden-schools-insight-idUSBRE9B905620131210

314. Cody, Anthony (Dec. 8, 2012). In Albuquerque, a Charter School that Recruits Dropouts? *Education Week/Teacher*. Retrieved from http://blogs.edweek.org/teachers/living-in-dialogue/2012/12/in_albuquerque_a_charter_schoo.html

315. Ravitch, Diane (Mar. 24, 2014). The Fatal Flaw of the Common Core Standards, *Diane Ravitch's blog*. Retrieved from http://dianeravitch.net/2014/03/24/the-fatal-flaw-of-the-common-core-standards/

316. Herold, Benjamin (Apr. 21, 2014). inBloom to Shut Down Amid Growing Privacy Concerns, *Education Week, Digital Education blog*. Retrieved from http://blogs.edweek.org/edweek/DigitalEducation/2014/04/inbloom_to_shut_down_amid_growing_data_privacy_concerns.html

317. Gilens, Martin and Page, Benjamin (Apr. 9, 2014). Testing Theories of American Politics: Elites, Interest Groups and Average Citizens. Retrieved from http://www.princeton.edu/~mgilens/Gilens homepage materials/Gilens and Page/Gilens and Page 2014-Testing Theories 3-7-14.pdf

318. Strauss, Valerie (Sep. 27, 2013). Bill Gates: 'It would be great if our education stuff worked, but…', *Washington Post/Answer Sheet*. Retrieved from http://www.washingtonpost.com/blogs/answer-sheet/wp/2013/09/27/bill-gates-it-would-be-great-if-our-education-stuff-worked-but/

319. The Danielson Group, *The Framework*. Retrieved July 31, 2014, from http://danielsongroup.org/framework/

320. Learning Sciences International, Introducing Dr. Marzano's Teacher Evaluation and Leadership Evaluation Model. Retrieved July 31, 2014, from http://www.marzanoevaluation.com/

321. Gould, Stephen Jay (1996). *Mismeasure of Man*, W. W. Norton & Co. http://www.amazon.com/Mismeasure-Man-Revised-Expanded/dp/0393314251

322. Koretz, Daniel (2009). *Measuring Up: What Educational Testing Really Tells Us*, Harvard University Press. http://www.amazon.com/Measuring-Up-Educational-Testing-Really/dp/0674035216

323. Harvard Graduate School of Education, A User's Guide to Peer Assistance and Review, Retrieved July 31, 2014, from http://www.gse.harvard.edu/~ngt/par/

324. Schneider, Mercedes (June 21, 2014). Transcript of Gates' March 2014 *Washington Post* Interview, *deutsch29 -- Mercedes Schneider's EduBlog*, Retrieved from http://deutsch29.wordpress.com/2014/06/21/transcript-of-gates-march-2014-washington-post-interview/

325. Strauss, Valerie (July 12, 2014). How Microsoft will make money from Common Core (in spite of what Bill Gates says) *Washington Post/Answer Sheet* blog, Retrieved from http://www.

washingtonpost.com/blogs/answer-sheet/wp/2014/07/12/how-microsoft-will-make-money-from-common-core-despite-what-bill-gates-said/

326. Gates, Bill (June 7, 2007). Remarks of Bill Gates, Harvard Commencement, 2007, *Harvard Gazette*. Retrieved from http://news.harvard.edu/gazette/story/2007/06/remarks-of-bill-gates-harvard-commencement-2007/

327. Measures of Effective Teaching Project. Retrieved July 31, 2014, from http://www.metproject.org

328. Gates, Bill (Dec. 9, 2008). Bill Gates Discusses Mayoral Control. [Video file]. Retrieved from https://www.youtube.com/watch?v=fSSYHj_6dXU

329. Weiss, Joanne (Mar. 31, 2011). The Innovation Mismatch: 'Smart Capital' and Education Innovation, *Harvard Business Review blog*. Retrieved from http://blogs.hbr.org/2011/03/the-innovation-mismatch-smart/

330. Ravitch, Diane (May 30, 2012). Why the Gates Compact? *Diane Ravitch's blog*. Retrieved from http://dianeravitch.net/2012/05/30/why-the-gates-compact/

331. Cody, Anthony (May 25, 2012). Payola Policy: NCTQ Prepares its Hit on Schools of Education, *Education Week/Teacher*. Retrieved from http://blogs.edweek.org/teachers/living-in-dialogue/2012/05/payola_policy_nctq_prepares_it.html

332. Center for Popular Democracy & Integrity in Education (May, 2014). Charter School Vulnerabilities to Waste, Fraud and Abuse. Retrieved from http://integrityineducation.org/charter-fraud/

333. Vogell, Heather (Sep. 28, 2013). Errors plague testing, hurt students in public schools, *MSN News*. Retrieved from http://news.msn.com/us/errors-plague-testing-hurt-students-in-public-schools/

334. Dillon, Sam (Aug. 5, 2010). Education Department Doles Out Big Awards, *New York Times*. Retrieved from http://www.nytimes.com/2010/08/05/education/05grants.html?_r=0

335. Darling-Hammond, Linda, et al (Feb. 29, 2012). Evaluating Teacher Evaluation, *Phi Delta Kappan/Education Week*, Retrieved from http://www.edweek.org/ew/articles/2012/03/01/kappan_hammond.html

336. Simon, Stephanie (Feb. 15, 2013). Special Report: Class Struggle – How charter schools get the students they want, *Reuters*. Retrieved from http://www.reuters.com/article/2013/02/15/us-usa-charters-admissions-idUSBRE91E0HF20130215

337. Kucsera, John (Mar. 26, 2014). New York State's Extreme School Segregation: Inequality, Inaction and a Damaged Future, *Civil Rights Project*. Retrieved from http://civilrightsproject.ucla.edu/research/k-12-education/integration-and-diversity/ny-norflet-report-placeholder

338. Paul, Annie Murphy (June 25, 2014). Educational technology isn't leveling the playing field, *Hechinger Report*. Retrieved from http://hechingerreport.org/content/educational-technology-isnt-leveling-playing-field_16499/

339. Cody, Anthony (June 30, 2014). Common Core-Aligned Tests and the New Pearson GED Test: Failure by Design? *Education Week/Teacher*. Retrieved from http://blogs.edweek.org/teachers/living-in-dialogue/2014/06/common_core-aligned_tests_and_.html

340. Associated Press (June 30, 2014). Gates says fixing education toughest challenge, *Mail Online*. Retrieved from http://www.dailymail.co.uk/wires/ap/article-2675817/Gates-says-fixing-education-toughest-challenge.html

341. Serrano, Ken (June 23, 2012). Massive college debt can burden graduates for decades. *USA Today*. Retrieved from http://usatoday30.usatoday.com/news/education/story/2012-06-24/college-debt-burdens-graduates/55784174/1

342. American Enterprise Institute (Mar. 13, 2014). From Poverty to Prosperity: A Conversation with Bill Gates. Retrieved from http://www.aei.org/files/2014/03/14/-bill-gates-event-transcript_082217994272.pdf

343. Newsnight: Jeremy Paxman challenges Bill Gates on tax (Jan. 23, 2014). [Video file]. Retrieved from https://www.youtube.com/watch?v=baUmdtrZp90

344. Goodell, Jeff (Mar. 13, 2014). Bill Gates: The Rolling Stone Interview, *Rolling Stone*. Retrieved from http://www.rollingstone.com/culture/news/bill-gates-the-rolling-stone-interview-20140313#ixzz36DvOM9uP

345. American Enterprise Institute (Mar. 13, 2014). From Poverty to Prosperity: A Conversation with Bill Gates. Retrieved from http://www.aei.org/files/2014/03/14/-bill-gates-event-transcript_082217994272.pdf

346. Pickett, Kate and Wilkinson, Richard, (2011). *The Spirit Level*, Bloomsbury Press. http://www.amazon.com/The-Spirit-Level-Equality-Societies/dp/1608193411

347. Burris, Carol (Aug. 12, 2013). How come officials could predict test results? *Washington Post/Answer Sheet* blog, Retrieved from http://www.washingtonpost.com/blogs/answer-sheet/wp/2013/08/12/how-come-officials-could-predict-results-on-new-test-scores/

348. Weber, Mark (Aug. 10, 2013). Scoring NY Tests With the Triple Lindy! *Jersey Jazzman*. Retrieved from http://jerseyjazzman.blogspot.com/2013/08/scoring-ny-tests-with-triple-lindy.html

349. Burris, Carol and Murphy, John (June 27, 2014). A disturbing look at Common Core tests in NY, *Washington Post/Answer Sheet* blog. Retrieved from http://www.washingtonpost.com/blogs/answer-sheet/wp/2014/06/27/a-disturbing-look-at-common-core-tests-in-new-york/

350. Diaz, Armando (Jan 2, 2014). New GED Test and Comprehensive New GED Program Launches Today, *GED Testing Service*, Retrieved from http://www.gedtestingservice.com/uploads/files/3abc4d490b455d0aafc7372a171927fd.pdf

About Anthony Cody

Born and raised in Berkeley, California, Anthony attended public schools there, and later graduated from UC Berkeley. His parents owned Cody's Books on Telegraph Ave, for many years one of the largest independent book stores on the West coast. He has two sons, now aged 22 and 24.

Social activism was a family value, and led Anthony to get his teaching credential in 1987, which he used to get a job teaching science at Bret Harte Middle School, where he taught for 18 years. In 2000, he became one of Oakland's first National Board certified teachers, and led district-wide efforts to strengthen science instruction.

In 2005 he left the classroom to become a Peer Assistance and Review "consulting teacher," working to help struggling teachers improve. In his next position, he headed a district-wide mentoring program designed to support beginning science teachers, called TeamScience.

His blog, Living in Dialogue, was launched at Education Week/ Teacher in 2008, and has won numerous awards, including a first place prize from the Education Writers Association in 2013. This blog has recently been reborn as an independent site, at www.livingindialogue. com. He created the Facebook community, Teachers' Letters to Obama, in 2009, and delivered strong messages of concern to the White House regarding the president's education policies.

In 2011, he was among the core organizers of the Save Our Schools March in Washington, DC, which brought more than 5000 protesters to the nation's capital. In 2013, he joined with Diane Ravitch to found the Network for Public Education, a national advocacy group that pushes for meaningful reform, and supports candidates willing to stand up for public schools.

In 2011, he retired from the Oakland schools after 24 years, and now lives in Mendocino County with his wife, two dogs and a cat named Pierre.